rom the

ur

The Bookman's Tale

BY THE SAME AUTHOR

A Treasonable Growth
Immediate Possession
The Age of Illusion
William Hazlitt: Selected Writings
Akenfield
The View in Winter
Writing in a War
Places: An Anthology of Britain
From the Headlands
The Short Stories of Ronald Blythe
Divine Landscapes
Private Words
Aldeburgh Anthology
Going to Meet George
Talking about John Clare
First Friends
The Assassin

The Wormingford Series

Word from Wormingford
Out of the Valley
Borderland
A Year at Bottengoms Farm
River Diary

The Circling Year
Talking to the Neighbours
A Writer's Day-book
Field Work: Collected Essays
Outsiders: A Book of Garden Friends

THE BOOKMAN'S TALE

RONALD BLYTHE

CANTERBURY
PRESS
Norwich

© Ronald Blythe 2009

First published in 2009 by the
Canterbury Press Norwich
Editorial office
13–17 Long Lane,
London EC1A 9PN, UK

Canterbury Press is an imprint of Hymns Ancient and Modern Ltd
(a registered charity)
St Mary's Works, St Mary's Plain,
Norwich NR3 3BH, UK

www.scm-canterburypress.co.uk

All rights reserved. No part of this publication may be reproduced,
stored in a retrieval system, or transmitted, in any form or by any
means, electronic, mechanical, photocopying or otherwise, without the
prior permission of the publisher, Canterbury Press.

The Author has asserted his right under the Copyright, Designs and
Patents Act, 1988, to be identified as the Author of this Work

British Library Cataloguing in Publication data

A catalogue record for this book is available
from the British Library

ISBN 978 1 85311 980 4

Printed and bound in Great Britain by
CPI Antony Rowe, Chippenham, Wiltshire

Contents

For Christine Smith

Foreword

These diary entries have mostly been taken from my 2007-08 Word from Wormingford column in *Church Times*, and I am grateful to Paul Handley for his kindness over many years. They include my farewell to my friend John Whale who died this year and who gave the column its title. Editing the sixth collection, I was struck by how much reading one does in the country, hence its title.

Ronald Blythe
Michaelmas, 2008

Hugh the Vet

Hugh the retired vet kindly bumps me down the ancient track in his gas-driven estate, and the tawny, or the brown, or the wood owl — it is the same bird — who dwells there suddenly sails before us in the January dusk.

Hugh says that a tawny owl sits nightly on his chimney and "bubbles". Gilbert White said that "most owls seemed to hoot exactly in B flat according to several pitch-pipes used in the tuning of harpsichords, and sold as strictly at concert pitch." They would descend from the Hanger and "sit hooting all night on my wall-nut trees. Their note is like a fine vox humana and very tuneable."

But listening to them hunting in the valley during the small hours, I hear a more archaic music, a wild and early sound. Hugh and I have had our wintry grumble about the state of England. All those new houses. All our old communities being doubled. And only a machine's turn, and never a hand's turn, on the farms.

But before long the talk comes back to creatures, wild or tamed, and all equal in the sight of Hugh. He loves them more than folk.

I remind him of the badger. Returning from a call in his always lofty vehicle — who knows? he might meet a needy elephant — his headlights pick out a run-over badger. He put it to sleep, placed it on the back seat, brought it to his surgery, sewed up its wounds, let it convalesce for a fortnight, and then drove it home to its wood. This very morning, he had untangled a muntjac from a wire fence.

I later informed the white cat of these great deeds, so that she should learn that men were more than waiters. She rolled on her back and eyed me lasciviously.

Soon it will be Twelfth Night, the end of euphoria, and Nemesis in the form of the credit card. The sofa-sellers have been yelling their heads off on TV. Buy, buy, buy — and with the idiotic 99 on every price-tag. A friend told me that these ads are purposely more decibelic than the programmes they interrupt.

Twelfth Night used to be a feast of misrule, when nothing and nobody was what it seemed to be. There was a brief turning of the tables, and an eating up of what could not be kept. Then came Plough Monday, and wet fields, and inescapable austerities that made those of Lent superfluous. A hard time we had of it.

They say it will snow. I visit the pointing bulbs in the cold beds, the fine young nettles in the wood, the pussy willow by the lake, the latter already near flowering, and cut some for the house. These little branches will not only bloom, but green. Thousands of snowdrops await their moment. The temperature shifts from cosy to arctic. The clouds are lowering and "full of it".

How we liked to know this "full of it" when we were children. Break, burst, let it all come down, wonderful, wonderful snow! Do not pity us. Block our lane, settle, drift, take over. Let us not tell road from field. Most probably, however, all that we shall get will be a white dusting of the winter wheat and the church mat. And so to the Epiphany, the light-filled time, the recognition time, the beautiful time.

Only a few weeks ago, Judy Rees, Margaret King, Vikram Seth, and I were walking the fields of Little Gidding. These had been heftily ploughed, but not yet harrowed. It was plainly autumn, and yet everything was equally plainly waiting for the poet's midwinter spring,

> When the short day is brightest,
>   with frost and fire,
> The brief sun flames the ice, on
>   pond and ditches,
> In windless cold that is the heart's
>   heat. . .

Christian Auden

One should always read a great poet's prose. There is usually plenty of it. W. H. Auden's is a long way from being crumbs from the banquet. I am devouring it in the garden — letters, essays, odds and ends.* And masses on his reading. He says, "Both Milton and Pope expect their audiences to consider their reading as a significant experience, comparable, say, to their falling in love." And much of Auden's reading is a falling in love with writers, novelists in particular. A lot of my youthful reading consisted of love affairs with suitable and unsuitable authors, Jeffrey Farnol, Denton Welch, Boswell, Marcel Proust . . . When I read of Auden's affair with Colette I rushed to the bookshelf to renew my acquaintance with Cheri.

What a truly good man Auden was. And what an all-round writer, working every morning until cocktail time at twelve-thirty, if only at the crossword. He lived through the dreadful fascist and Stalinist heresies, firmly and unapologetically holding on to his family tradition of Church of England parsons. He insisted that they were High Anglicans, not Anglo-Catholics, emphasising the difference. Neither the words nor the music of this Church ever left him. They sang in his heart. He loved its inclusivity and he saw himself as the child of a fine faith. His guru was Kierkegaard, his saviour was Christ. The Christ of the English industrial Midlands of his boyhood who would walk with him through all the triumphs and fame and sufferings of his life.

He describes this faith with candour: "I was lucky enough to be born in a period when every educated person was expected to know the Bible thoroughly and no undergraduate could take a degree without passing a Divinity examination." And he goes on, as we all fretfully do, about today's scripture illiteracy, and thus the near-impossibility of young people discovering the riches of the faith. In a modern parish, Auden means.

Like many poets of his time Auden had to make a livelihood out of lecturing and reviewing, and like them he did not possess a lesser language for his journeywork. Thus he wrote and spoke well, even brilliantly, and with a brave political fervour and great morality. His homosexual lovers were unfaithful, his celebrity was a burden, but always there was this paradise of literature, these bound friends and acquaintances piled up around him. Writing about them for money could have been necessary jobbery in order to write his poetry, but his criticism and letters, and lectures bear no sign of being a lesser task. On the contrary these things show a huge enjoyment and wit which are catching, so that I wanted to read for the first time, or read afresh, the books he mentions.

What I noticed most was that this is uncomputerised prose. There is a difference. Prose written with a pen and then typed-up, a fag dangling from the lip. It went into *The New Yorker* and *The New York Times*, into introductions to the classics, into the heads of readers, never to escape. He wrote, "Every work of art is an answer to the same unformulated question: 'Who goes there?' and its answer is always: 'Me'."

* *The complete Works of W. H. Auden: Prose, Vol. III, 1949-1955*, edited by Edward Mendelson, Princeton University Press.

George Herbert's Sickness

Outside it is April in January, with snowdrops climbing the graves and starlings rushing over. Inside, we crowd into the chancel so that we can truthfully sing, "Lord, we are few, but thou art near."

Falls of Garrya — named in honour of Nicholas Garry of the Hudson Bay Company — tumble from the sanctuary vases. Through its representatives, the village is at prayer. Everyone knows what to do and does it perfectly, and I am like one of those conductors whose arms go up and down in front of those who know the piece backwards. Yet prayer happens. I feel it happening.

Christ's friends, good Jews that they were, prayed on and off throughout each day, like our good Muslims. But when they saw him praying they said, "Lord, teach us how to pray."

My praying for the past two months was all about cancer. Five friends had been diagnosed with five different kinds of it. I wrote a list, and went through it each prayer-time. And it made me think of George Herbert, a young man suffering from consumption, the "cancer" of his day.

I remembered his less-than-three years' ministry in what must have been a church and rectory-like building sites for a good part of his occupation, and with "death puffing at the door" or "working like a mole" in his thin body. So surely there must be some desperate consumption prayer like my consuming cancer prayers? But there is not.

Like the flowers he adored, he wrote, "I follow straight without complaints or grief." Sometimes his spirit is "lost in flesh", and he notes how "life retains us from God." All the same, he loves being alive, loves playing his lute, loves writing, loves singing in Salisbury Cathedral over the water-meadows.

There are bad moments. Yet "now in age I bud again After so many deaths I live and write." Very ill, he says, "Lord, make my losses up and set me free." Another dear Cambridge friend, centuries later, asked the same request when I sat with her. It could have been those dreadful fens that "did" for Herbert. The whole University coughed with their "ague".

In "The Size", he matches the familiar portrait we have of him with a self-description.

A Christian's state and case
Is not corpulent, but a thinne and spare,
Yet active strength: whose long and bonie face
Content and care
Do seem to equally divide,
Like a pretender, not a bride.

Herbert took great care not to have any truck with the doctors of his day, and treated himself with what we would call alternative medicine. "Herbs gladly cure our flesh; because that they Find their acquaintance there." But Christ is his ultimate

All-heal (Prunella vulgaris). Talking to Christ made him instantly better.

And so, instead of being a plea for a cure or an autobiography of illness, his poetry is a holy conversation-piece in which we are occasionally allowed to join in. Of course, there are ups and downs. "One ague dwelleth in my bones Another in my soul," but the latter is soon cured. He had only to pray (talk) and the healthy conversation would begin.

Tobias and the Sitter

Toby the artist has arrived from Swanage to paint my portrait. He looks round the old house for the "best sitting place" and chooses the study window. Rainy panes flash with intermittent sunshine.

Toby is working on a series of portraits of rural people, mostly from Wessex, whose way of life is being destroyed by those who most admire it — the incomers. "Each man kills the thing he loves." Or, as a Dorset hurdle-maker told Toby, referring to the new race of village-dwellers, "they love what they see and then they change it to what they left behind."

He draws and paints for three days, and I hope is impressed by my professionalism as an artist's model, as I manage to chat and provide meal-breaks without moving, so to speak. And, of course, it is a treat to be in Dorset once more. It was Paul Nash's favourite place, and I myself made wonderful trips to it when I was helping to edit the New Wessex edition of Thomas Hardy, or writing about T. F. Powys. Or climbing Maiden Castle.

We talk about the way in which, not all that long ago, local people could get trapped in landscape: how it could destroy them, as it did in *The Return of the Native*.

Tall and serious, Toby paints away while the white cat, new to the smell of turpentine, considers this change of environment. My face, along with the hurdle-maker's and those of all the other country men and women who will sit for him, will hang in the Dorset County Museum in Dorchester.

This is an extraordinary institution, possessing, as it does, Thomas Hardy's study in a room-sized glass case. He used a different pen, I remember, for each novel, writing on its holder *Tess of the D'Urbervilles*, *The Woodlanders*, etc. But how strange that this most furtive of authors should have his very soul on display! Not that I wasn't glued to the glass when I entered the museum at "seeing" not only the worn nibs, but the inky fingers pressing on, line after line, and the blotter working overtime.

Toby says that he has bought a boat named Selina and would like to change this, but it is unlucky. Ships are never re-christened. Which brings us to Tobias and the angel, and myself to sorting out Jacob and his angel, and the completely forgotten tale of Tobit, Tobias, and Raphael. This is well worth anyone's glimpse of the Apocrypha.

Briefly, Tobit, a Jewish exile in Nineveh and blind, allows his son to travel with a guide named Azarius, who is in fact the angel Raphael.

Off they go, to Tobias's mother's grief, to find fish, which will provide the means for her son's happy marriage and her husband's sight. And, of course, Tobias has a dog, Dog Toby.

It is a great tale. I take the artist Tobias to see a portrait by John Constable at Nayland, just up the road, the model for which was his brother Golding, a young land agent. He stares upwards as the Christ, a natural-enough gesture for him, as he was usually walking through the Suffolk woods with his gun. Then back to the sitting.

It is etiquette not to remark on a work in progress or even to look at it. But when Tobias at last turns the canvas round, I am disconcerted by how far he has seen into me, and how correctly. And how truthful even my chair is! Off he goes in the wild, wild weather, the easel folded up in the car like a sleeping insect.

The Dig above Smallbridge Hall

Just below the farmhouse, where everything — stream, lane, and field — takes a sharp right turn, there are indelible marks of occupation. Just an overgrown tangle and a brick or two, nothing more. A double-dweller stood there in a stingy garden. Poor labouring folk, men, women, and children, clung to life on its few square yards. One of the boys went to Gallipoli. All the girls went into service.

The double-dweller emptied and tottered, fell down. Nettles grew their stinging comment over it. It retained its breath — that unmistakable odour of human settlement. One draws it in from places many times older than a Victorian cottage, from a ring-dwelling on Bodmin moor, from the wintering glades of gypsies.

I could almost hear the Gaelic singing when I sat in the huge silence of the deserted village at Rannoch when I picked up artefacts on the Smallbridge land. I touched the warm hands that had chipped away at them.

A long time ago, Alan and I walked through Bunyan, and

came to his birthplace. It was exactly like the site of the double-dweller at home. Although here was greatness, not obscurity, the faintness of the habitation was similar.

We stood there, imagining the Bedfordshire boy knocking the mud off his boots, collecting firewood, and setting up sticks to play Tipcat. The Bunyans had lived here for generations, and had come down in the world. "For my descent, then, it was, as is well known by many, of a low and inconsiderable generation, my father's house being of that rank at its meanest and most despised of all the families in the land."

But, attending Bedford Grammar School, Bunyan would have had as good an education as Shakespeare, and, along with his friend Harry, he would have had all the fun in the world, from dancing to bell-ringing. But, as Alan and I realised, Bunyan's birth plot must still be among the least-altered surroundings of any great writer. Thus his presence "hit me" as I touched a piece of red tile, and watched a stream from Harrowden Road bend its way to the great Ouse. Bunyan drank from this stream, and went under the water, like Christ, in the cold river.

Archaeologists are at work above the Stour. Elizabeth I had hunted, or watched the hunt, in the deer-park below, and they may have discovered her pavilion. She would have viewed our church, but not my house as it skulked in its watery hide.

"Oh, we knew it was there!" said the old chaps. They meant the hunting lodge. In an ancient village, no sight goes unseen, no mark goes unmeditated. After the Second World War, a dozen or more cottages were destroyed — some put a match to — on the grounds of slum clearance. These are now mourned, not as the old homesteads, but as the short-sighted destruction of estate agents' dreams.

The poet John Clare perversely — to some — loved his rough

birthplace. He was made ill by an enforced move to a far better house. My ancient Suffolk birthplace was accidentally burnt down, thatch, beams, and all, and one of those popular village signs on posts now marks the spot. It shows the brass of Sir Robert de Bures, which was so loved by rubbers that they now have to take its impression from a facsimile. But I glance at it from the bus, and at the mown grass, and at the modern bungalows, and realise how much less there is of "me" on this spot, and of the farm labourers or Bunyan on their spots.

Monk Talk

News from a far country came, i.e. Washington. It gives me the latest on St Anselm's Abbey on South Dakota Avenue, where my friend Dom Gabriel, who, as one would hope, writes like an angel, lives according to the Benedictine Rule.

Dom Peter, the headmaster, spends his days listening, praying, calming, urging, convincing, encouraging. Dom Daniel, a quiet man, listens. Dom Philip is a study in energy and movement, and holds forums with Buddhist, Hindu, and Sikh communities.

Dom Edward is on loan from Downside Abbey and is "in the richest sense of the word" a cosmopolite. Dom Boniface paints icons. Dom James has been backpacking in the Sierra Nevada and writing about Thomas Merton. Dom Christopher has been having a six-month sabbatical in Wales.

Dom Simon says "that the more we entrust ourselves to God and to a life lived in faith, the more our mind sees, and our heart expands, preparing us to erupt one day into eternal life". Abbot

Alban is 96 and says that he is grateful for "all of it". Dom Hilary is excellent on the website, and loves the liturgy. Dom Dunstan, "our sole Canadian", has been travelling and teaching in Korea.

Dom Matthew is a guest-master and a definite and a benevolent presence, but a pre-monastic Manhattanite. Dom Edmund teaches physics and "is a kind of legend". Dom Dominic is bursar, cantor, and on loan from Saint Louis. Dom Michael is sub-prior and master of ceremonies, archivist, and polymath — "But now my cell is much smaller, my days more predictable, my time more flexible, my prayer more wide-ranging."

Lastly, my old friend Dom Gabriel, who is exploring hymns for vespers, or searching out new music for the eucharist, or in all probability reading Barbara Pym, or biking, or listening to Bach.

Were I even slightly community-minded, I would envy these monks. But, as Dom Gabriel knows, I cannot imagine it. We met in Hereford ages ago when I gave a lecture on Kilvert, and was seated next to Miss Kilvert, the diarist's niece.

It was when I told him of a correspondence I had with Barbara Pym. Talk about "And did you once see Shelley plain?" How his eyes lit up. And so, every end of the year, he tells me about his abbey, and I think about them all and marvel at their closeness and goodness and cleverness on broad South Dakota Avenue.

An English monk, Edward Crouzet OSB, wrote about the polarisation of American Roman Catholics. "Early on I encountered the two poles in the celebration of the mass. On the first occasion, as celebrant myself, I was invited to sit in a circle of sisters on cushion chairs, the altar a low table, the chalice ceramic, the homily a dialogue, the intercessions spontaneous, the sign of peace fulsome and lengthy, communion passed from hand to hand.

"On the second, attending mass as a member of the congregation one weekend at the nearest church to where I was staying, I encountered a *missa normativa* in Latin, with the priest facing east although the altar was free-standing, no sign of peace, communion on the tongue, many of the women in black hats or mantillas, the music beautifully performed by a polyphonic choir.

Though I hesitate to admit it, I actually enjoyed both experiences. Each pole is committed to its vision of the Church. What is sad is that the commitment is so exclusive. They talk about, but never to, each other."

I am off to talk about post-Christmas carols.

Antony and Our Lady

Ash Wednesday. Mighty drifts of snowdrops, more than I have ever seen before. They cover the old stackyard, flowering between the dead nettle stalks, run through the wood, and fill up the beds. Tenby (*Obvallaris*) daffodils have come out in the orchard.

Defrosting the fridge, I discover an icy foot of something that turns out to be a trout. So a correct liturgical supper.

Racing skies and thin sunshine. On the radio, howling and shrieking at the hustings, as Hillary, Barack, and John invoke their mothers. They have mothers? Gosh.

The previous Wednesday, Antony arrived from Walsingham, and I took him to Sudbury to show him the shrine of our Lady.

It was made by two Walsingham craftsmen, James and Lilian Dagless, for the Roman Catholic church in Sudbury. The priest at that time, Fr Moir, reinstated it — and his mother, a Protestant, paid for it.

My mother thought he should have been hanged for doing this, although not drawn and quartered, as she was a devout Christian.

The Virgin and Child, covered in gold leaf, and she in a Mary-blue robe, glitter beneath a canopy. They were carried in procession from the banks of the Stour to the chapel (then a barn) of St Bartholomew. This on the Feast of the Assumption. "Well," said Mother, "you would think we were in Italy!"

The shrine's original home was in the marvellous collegiate church of St Gregory a few yards up the river bank. It was where I worshipped as a boy, and where my sister was married. It has a glorious telescopic font cover from the late Middle Ages. On Ash Wednesday, curtains would have been hung from its dizzy finials. Antony, seeing it for the first time, is moved by its beauty, touching the still-bright scarlet of apostle-less niches gently, recognising its holiness as I recognise its history.

To the south of the church, the porch and the chapel of St Anne, the Virgin's mother, are conjoined. This is where the shrine of our Lady originally stood, but where a pair of vast aldermanic tomb-chests now take up the space: Alderman Carter, no less, whose charity they proclaim. "This day" — in Latin — "a Sudbury camel passed through the eye of the Needle."

A grander local benefactor, Archbishop Simon of Sudbury, had founded a college here in 1375. One of its miserere seats, its arms as smooth as silk from the resting palms of centuries, clunks upwards to reveal the Archbishop's beloved dog. I used to wonder if it sat at his feet in church. Alas, poor local lad, he came a cropper over the poll tax, and was beheaded by the mob during the Peasants' Revolt.

The head gazes through the glass of one of those hatches such as used to be seen in ticket offices, and is irreverently known as "the nut" by choirboys. But I am profoundly moved by it, by its sightless elegance, and its huge fate. Did his colleague carry it from its spike in London to his church in Sudbury out of love, or in the hope that it would do for Sudbury what that other murdered archbishop did for Canterbury? Antony stares at this eloquent skull in his quiet thinking way.

Outside, gulls whirl above the river. Did Simon swim in it? He had crowned the boy king Richard II. Like many East Anglians, he was naturally radical. Events — office — did for him.

Fr Hugh Rose and the Oxford Movement

A week of proper toil as was fit for Lent 1. At the desk all morning with the sun hot on my back; in the garden all the afternoon with the sun fit for summer. My conscience struggles between global warming and bliss.

Thousands of flowers are in bloom. The days pull out, as they say in the village. And the oil runs out. When I confess this to the oilman I receive a scolding. "You're the 21st [fool, I thought he was about to say] customer to have said that to me today."

Soon, the special little tanker for tracks like mine creeps to the house, and soon the surprisingly bitterly cold rooms grow cosy. In church, I preach on the nature of deserts. They were burning all day and shivering all night. Those voluminously robed figures who cross and recross our screen every hour tell of sheltering from heat and chill for centuries. Cover up.

It is midwinter, and I am dressed like Monty Don in India, as I dig and cut in jeans and shirt. And it is, as nobody can stop saying, February.

Middle-aged friends arrive, and every half-hour one or other of their mobiles rings. They dive into handbag or pocket and say, "Excuse me," and walk a little ahead or a little behind. All this about a dozen times. "Escape me? Never!" say the mobiles. In between, we talk about art.

If one goes to a concert or to Westminster Abbey, one has to silence one's mobile. Should not this be the etiquette when out to lunch or on a country walk? We are in an age, however, when few of us can bear to switch off whatever happens to be switched on. I heard a funny play about this on Radio 4. A woman couldn't switch off Radio 4. A demobilised artist friend paints to loud Verdi.

Persistent questioning at a literary festival forced me to admit that I often wrote with a pen. In vain did I try to show a kind of advancement in my medium by telling the audience that Iris Murdoch and Ivy Compton-Burnett and Wilfred Owen used a pencil. As for the telephone, I use it sparingly, with the result that it rings sparingly.

During an amiable talk at the local history society, the pencilled profile of Fr Hugh Rose suddenly enlivens the screen, riveting my full attention. I had frequently wondered what he looked like. He looked like Wordsworth. He was one of those Anglican priests who, like Herbert, haven't all that much time to do what they were born to, dying at 43.

In 1830, he accepted the Archiepiscopal Peculiar living of Hadleigh, Suffolk, disturbing its torpor. Rationalised religious philosophisings were being debated in Germany and, for some people, threatening traditional Christianity. What to do? Fr Hugh called the Hadleigh Conference, which in turn sparked the Oxford Movement.

There was a fine brick Tudor tower in his rectory garden, and there W. Palmer, A. P. Perceval, and R. H. Froude set the seeds of Tractarianism.

A previous Hadleigh priest was my boyhood hero — Rowland Taylor, the Marian martyr, burnt on the common in 1555. During his brief time there, Hugh Rose erected a wordy obelisk on the spot. I would prop my bike against its railings and imagine the terrible scene, the fat old man from Northumbria who had listened to Erasmus at Cambridge, and the horrible magistrate from over the fields who had slapped his face for saying his last psalm in English. And now the gentle Hugh the unifier.

The Watcher by the Beehive

The old friend takes up her position at the crossroads. Warmly wrapped, contemplative, familiar, she watches the world go by. One road leads to where General Fairfax stationed his troops during the Civil War, one to the little priory that a Saxon couple founded, one to Duncan's farm and to me, and one to the river. Perched also at the crossroads are the Beehive pub and the letter-box.

Not so very long ago the village — every village — peered out through lace curtains. Its patron saint was Miss Marple, Queen of Nosiness. But the TV has changed all this. Not only does it reveal far more interesting happenings than the window, but it has created an indifference to local morals.

Only 20 years ago, a landowner refused to let a cottage to an unmarried couple. Now, they could live any way they liked as long as they paid the rent. The Church, too, ceases to poke about in people's private lives. The old, rich, wicked, ruinous gossip that made life hell (and enthralling) is not so much silenced as given a more acceptable language.

But, in any case, say what you will, the gadgetry of the age — television, computers, cars, mobiles, not to mention the Freedom of Information Act — has turned parish scandal and eccentricity into something that one has to be adult about. These recent inventions have certainly wrecked rural fiction. Think of secrets like Lady Dedlock's or Mr Rochester's. The Archers' scriptwriters have their work cut out to keep Brian disgraceful. A love-child — gosh!

But the old lady sits by the crossroads, preserving, in the highest sense, the rural tradition of watching. It is good to see her. I sit out a great deal, and the horses, cat, and birds watch me. And, at weekends, the ramblers and the dog servants. "There he was," they will mention to their families when they get home, stamping my mud off, "sitting outside with a book."

Our ancestors were so eager to observe the world go by their dwelling-places that they built them as near to the highway as was safe. A cart, a young traveller, pilgrims, Gypsies, a bagman, a carriage, endless children, passers-by with whom to pass the time of day. If you lived in town, preferably in the busiest streets, bow windows like opera boxes would give full view of the drama of human existence.

Abraham was sitting outside his tent, an old man and deserving of simply "looking", when he saw three walkers. It was hot. Company at last! He could not do enough for them. The scene always reminds me of James Boswell and Dr Johnson on their Scottish tour. How they would send their servant ahead of them to Lord Monboddo, for example, longing for guests in his castle, lonely, bored. Then, "Dr Samuel Johnson is on his way!" And the joyful preparation. Nothing too much trouble for the passer-by.

Ancient Abraham ran to the approaching visitors. "Let a little water be fetched and wash your feet, and rest yourselves under the tree," and to Sarah, "Make cakes upon the hearth." She was inside the tent when she heard the travellers tell her husband that she would have a son. She laughed. The things people said when they walked by one's door! When they sat under one's tree!

"Put 'To John' "

"A man that looks on glass, on it may stay his eye" and see how badly the kitchen window needs cleaning. It is my 6 a.m. meditation come News, come the white cat to sit on me, come the plans for the day.

The moneychangers are in free fall on the radio; the lawyers are busy with ridiculous people. But the spring sun spins along the horizon, and the horses provide elegant silhouettes on the top field. "Sweet day, so cool, so calm, so bright." The river is in flood after last Sunday's 24-hour rain.

There are black and white lambs. There are little cries. A wren tumbles through the budding climbing rose. I read the psalm for Wednesday in Holy Week, "Hear, O thou Shepherd of Israel, thou that leadest Joseph like a sheep: shew thyself also, thou that sittest upon the cherubims. . . Turn us again, thou God of hosts." It goes on:

"O let us live." What an enchanting poem.

Toast jumps from the toaster, and the cat jumps through the flap to find out what is going on outside. One day, when I am very old, I will mourn, then celebrate a time like this, not attending services, but reading a window.

A drive to the Woodbridge bookshop to sign books. The Stour flashes white and silver. The customers say, "Put 'To John'," "Put 'To Mrs Smith'." For 20 years, I cycled into this Suffolk town to pick up things that I couldn't get at the village shop. I would walk by the Deben and in March see the boat-builder, the yachtsmen scraping away, the seabirds being whirled over Sutton Hoo.

The bookseller, Martin, says, "Choose something for your-self," and I choose Ted Hughes's *Letters*, remembering when he and I unveiled a tablet to John Clare in Westminster Abbey, and he had read "The Nightingale's Rest", and we had all sung Clare's

A Man there lived in Galilee
Unlike all men before,
For he alone from first to last
Our flesh unsullied wore;
A perfect life of perfect deeds
Once to the world was shown,
That all mankind might mark his steps
And in them plant their own.

Kevin Crossley-Holland and his wife come to tea. He has to sign books at the Wivenhoe bookshop. It is "Writers, awake!"

Find a good pen. They have brought me an extravagant Easter cake and put it by the tin containing my hot cross buns; for everything must be devoured in its proper season. We talk about his translation of the ancient poem *The Dream of the Rood*, made when he was 23, and long a favourite of mine. The Cross itself gives us a first-hand account of its part in the death of Christ. It is a tree eyewitness.

Kevin says that the poet would have been familiar with Holy Week liturgy and its magnificent Latin hymns "The royal banners forward go" and "Sing, my tongue, the glorious battle". It is conceivable that so did the royalty of Sutton Hoo. I imagine those voices over the Deben.

Art and Weather

"It was not always like this," I admonish the white cat: "tinned breakfast regularly at six, gorgeous radiators, blackbirds through the window, devoted old chap." Sometimes I hear them, the skinny labourers clumping down from the bothy to feed the stock, the girls singing in the dairy, the barefoot children falling over the dogs, the mother shouting, the pot bubbling. All gone into the dark, says the poet. Or into the light, says somebody else.

Easter lilies are trumpeting in freezing churches, good for at least a month. Easter Anthems — "page 165 in the green book" — are sung, have died away. We have trudged all the way to Emmaus for the feast. On the farm both the corn and the "rubbish", i.e. all the wild and lovely things, are springing up. In the churchyard, a stone has been taken away to have Gordon's name carved on it. In the great ditch, there are wild garlic, dog's mercury, and bluebell stubs all over again.

Marina Warner and I have returned from shepherding some university students round the Constable country in a downpour. We stand and steam by the fire. In East Bergholt churchyard, we called on the artist's parents, his father Golding and his mother Anne, Willy Lott, and the Dunthornes. It was Mr Dunthorne, plumber and glazier and house painter, who had shown the teenage Constable how to mix his colours. And it was young Jonny Dunthorne who had set himself up as picture-cleaner, and who had scrubbed Rubens's mighty *Château du Steen*.

In Dedham Church, we peered up at Constable's beautiful Christ, who may have been modelled by the doorkeeper of the Royal Academy, an ex-soldier and ex-village choirboy, for whom the artist found a job after the Napoleonic wars.

The steep lane to Flatford Mill was a water-course, an added river. My brother and I used to whizz down it on our bikes, John Nash in his Triumph Herald, on the way to the flower-painting class, with his model, a single bloom from the garden, leaping on the dashboard.

What with our dogs rushing about with joy and people sticking wet mobiles in their ears, and the sheer muddle that downpours set up, nobody takes much notice of my lecture. I tell the wind: "This is where *The Cornfield* is set; this is where he painted *Boat Building on the River Stour, The Haywain* . . ." Dogs rejoice. No one complains. Marina sploshes along, staying wonderfully elegant in her long coat. "John Constable was the most weathered of all the artists of his day. He could paint rain."

It was Jesus who drew his friends' attention to the equality of rain. It fell on the just and the unjust. Shakespeare likened it to the inescapability of mercy. I am devoted to it, though not when I have to talk through it.

I think of the tramping Jesus in all weathers, him and his friends either scorched or soaked. I imagine them sheltering, their hair dripping, their robes clinging, the sandy mud squelching between "those feet". O for Bethany and one of Martha's meals!

And now it is Wednesday in Easter Week, and we must read Luke's last words. "These are the words which I spake unto you while I was yet with you. . ." So pay attention. Let them not be rained off.

Walking in Edinburgh

They say that one's life streams past one when drowning, but so a good stretch of it is apt to do on the Kings Cross-Edinburgh line. It is a sullen April day, with wheeling birds and low crops, but there is Helpston Church and John Clare's whole world, "a gloomy village in Northamptonshire, on the brink of the Lincolnshire fens". His words, not mine.

And here is York, with its brilliant, port-holed station, and here, though gone in a second, is Durham, into which I carried my baby godson, good as gold, past the Venerable Bede and St Cuthbert.

And there, for miles and miles, is the sacred shore of Northumberland. And here come the Borders, where illiterate sheep-rustlers fought like heroes and became lords. And here, all of a sudden, comes Waverley Station — and some staggeringly cold air when I leave the carriage. Princes Street whirls and dances in snowflakes.

Walking to George Street, I glimpse Rose Street, where the post-war poets drank themselves into bouts of genius, my friend George Mackay Brown among them. And then the George Hotel and its shelter.

Breakfast is the best hotel meal. It is lavish, interesting, leisurely. Showered businessmen, crackling newspapers, considerate comings and goings, greedy old couples, sleepy lovers, suits and ties and bare-armed girls, and beautiful waitresses learning the language.

I eat an awful lot. More toast, more coffee, more warm hotel, more guests to stare and wonder at. A pair of scaffolders arrive from on high. Might they have some breakfast? Yes, yes. Sausages, bacon, egg, black pudding, fruit, marmalade, juice for all mankind. But no Scotch porridge.

Then out into the bitter weather. Except that the sun is playing on the vast architecture, and warming up the wind. And the smell of Scotland, heather, water, and a kind of ancient grandeur blowing through the city.

Alice meets me in the National Gallery, where I have to give a lecture on artists from the Suffolk-Essex countryside. But, before this, I have had time to call on the paintings I first met in my 20s — Gainsborough's Mrs Graham, poor St Sebastian being tied up for his martyrdom, a lovely Paul Nash — and to sit on one of those buttoned couches that are perfectly placed for drowsing in front of masterpieces.

Although, to be fair to myself, I could not be more awake; for this is what Scotland does to me: gets the blood flowing — presumably so I won't collapse with hypothermia and create a public nuisance on the Doric steps. The truth is that never have I felt so healthy.

To prove it, I visit all the museums from the Castle to Holy-rood Palace, exploring every close, wandering into St Giles's Kirk, seeing the early tourists from Japan, having some conversation with a fine cat, and walking about ten miles — it seems. Nowhere else in Britain is the dangerous hugger-mugger of late-medieval/early-modern town existence so emotionally retained as in Edinburgh.

From the poky, tragic rooms of Mary Queen of Scots to the warren that is the Royal Mile, "early skyscraper", one hardly needs to be Sir Walter Scott or Robert Louis Stevenson to feel the past passionately accompanying one wherever one goes.

Back home, at matins, I remembered Scotland by choosing Psalm 122 from the Scottish Psalter — "Therefore I wish that peace may still Within thy walls remain."

Lark's Voice

A warm spring morning. I wheel the old newspapers up the farm track for the dustman, two-thirds of them unread. Helpless we are before the waste. But the larks! It is father's birthday. He would have been 110, an April boy.

Returning, the skylarks cover me with their song. Two of them? An entire lark quintet? The music is high and glorious. But the Big Field is used to it. Decade after decade, since Edmund or whoever it was, these dizzy birds in the blue air making a singing canopy for the early toilers. A pair of devoutly married magpies, tremendously handsome, add a couple of low notes. But chiefly it is larks. They are invisible to the admiring eye.

One thing I did read in the paper was that Vaughan

Williams's *The Lark Ascending* remains our most popular piece of music. But it is now journalistically correct to bewail an absence of larks. Where do these people live? Poets strive against each other to sing the lark, Tennyson with his "sightless song", and John Clare to his Jane, "The lark's in the grass love, Building her nest"; so we know what is on his mind.

Lark's voice, says my bird conductor, "A clear, liquid 'chir-r-up' song, a high-pitched, musical outpouring, very long sustained, in hovering and descending flight, and occasionally from the earth or a low perch." So skylarks do not even need the sky. As feathered music, they can be grounded or ethereal. The trouble with skylarks is that they refuse to allow ornithology to cage them. Off they wing into human art the moment they open their mouths, theirs clearly being the song of songs, as the Psalmist puts it, "in the house of our pilgrimage". And so I loiter to listen to it all over again, the song of the Big Field larks as it fills the universe.

John Clare now and then put his Northamptonshire skylarks in their place — "a bird that is of as much use in poetry as the nightingale". But then, being Clare and village naturalist-extraordinary, he writes as follows: "The skylark is a slender light bird with a coppled crown on the head [and] builds its nest on the ground and lays five or six spotted eggs. This is the one celebrated by poets for the sweetness of its song. They gather in flocks after harvest and are caught in some parts by nets, thrown at nights in great quantities. A redcap lives about seven years in a cage, a skylark about 14. I knew of one kept tame by a publican at Tallington."

It was on an April day like this that John Clare read in his local paper, the *Stamford Mercury*, that "The Lingfield and Crowhurst choir sung several select pieces from Handel in the cavity of the Yew tree in the churchyard of the latter place. The tree is 36 feet in circumference and is now in a growing state — The hollow was fitted up like a room and sufficiently large to contain the performers — On clearing out the interior of the tree some years ago a 7lb cannon ball was discovered which had no doubt been fired into it. . ."

There is a vast oak in my track which would have been standing then (1820), hollow in parts, though nowhere wide enough to hold even a flautist. But a great many creatures dwell in it. It drinks from a brook. I think of the Lord in springtime and his bird-music.

The Limits of our Seeing

It is the Eve of the Ascension, and dashing rains and streaky sunbeams take turns to soak the house. Oaks are out before ash; therefore we shall have a splash. Duncan and two other men are moving the white ribbon that allows the horses to eat their way across the hill in an orderly fashion. It is very chilly, and to-morrow will be May Day.

I have returned from Peter's funeral — Peter the storyteller and practical joker, much loved, much missed. Wet winds whipped our robes around us, and the earth let in one more poor body, and what we still call "the sky" let in one more dear soul.

The congregation drives away to the village hall for the bake-meat, or tea as it is now called, and I drop off at the village shop to buy Felix for one whose need is greater than mine. Stitch-wort and Coca-Cola tins decorate the ditch.

I think of the post-resurrection appearances as a mighty sculptor created them on a tympanum at Vézelay: Christ's meeting the Marys, his walk to Emmaus, and finally his leave-taking on the Mount of Olives, all in whirling stone; and I hear his greetings and farewells.

The tympanum fills the space above the church door and that of the inner ear. The Paschal candle will be snuffed on Ascension Day, his light filling the universe, "And the portals high are lifted To receive their heavenly King" — Christopher Wordsworth, the poet's brother. But I especially like Mrs Alexander's

And ever on our earthly path
A gleam of glory lies,
A light still breaks behind the cloud
That veils thee from our eyes.

And I especially love the marvellous *The Cloud of Unknowing*, which is required reading for Ascension Day. Clifton Wolters, its translator, suggests that it may have been written by an East Midlands country parson during the terrible and yet devotionally wonderful 14th century, when Black Death and war "lost", as it were, to the great mystics Julian of Norwich, Richard Rolle, and Walter Hilton. And, at Ascensiontide especially, to an East Midlands country parson, who could write like this:

"Do not think that because I call it a 'darkness' or a 'cloud' it is the sort of cloud you see in the sky, or the kind of darkness you know at home when the light is out. That kind of darkness or cloud you can picture in your mind's eye in the height of summer, just as in the depth of a winter's night you can picture a clear and shining light. I do not mean this at all.

"By 'darkness' I mean 'a lack of knowing' — just as anything you do not know or may have forgotten may be said to be dark to you, for you cannot see it with your inward eye. For this reason it is called a 'cloud', not of the sky, of course, but of 'unknowing', a cloud of unknowing between you and God."

The friends of Jesus on the Vézelay carving are looking downwards at what they have to do now that he has ascended and left them in charge. They look practical, and he looks not unlike a small bird winging its way home.

Mont Bures — Kohima

The last day of the midwinter spring, and a confirmation at Mount Bures.

Apple blossom shudders in the cold. A pair of ancient bells — *Sancte Necolae Ora Pro Nobis* and *Sit Nomen Domini Benedictum* — jangle across the fields. Bread and wine by the altar, chocolate cake by the font. Henry the Vicar in his stall, the tall Bishop and I on the chancel step, the candidates on their kneelers, and the gentle, firm drawing in of them into the Church.

Chris at the chamber organ. The little girl, the young ladies, the even-taller-than-the-Bishop young man are, to quote the book, admitted to the Church of the Redeemed and sealed to eternal life and the imparting of the Spirit. The Bishop has the gift of doing and saying all this as though it had never been done before.

Once upon a time, baptism and confirmation took place together. Henry VIII brought his daughter Elizabeth to this double entry into the Church when she was three days old. Some believe that the fullness of the Holy Spirit is imparted at baptism. School chaplains now take great care that confirmation should not become confused with a puberty rite. My learned informant says: "The complexity of the evidence is such as to suggest that a final solution will not be reached by an appeal to history."

As nobody has been confirmed at Mount Bures during the past 60 years, the little hilltop church feels as if it is being drawn back into something mysterious — something that was there, but waiting to re-express itself. Thousand-year-old churches say difficult things. You need your religious wits about you to catch their drift.

Afterwards to the Colonel's house by the river, to the long descent from the Mount to see photographs of Kohima, where they laid a red carpet for him. There he is, upright and bemused, our neighbour and their hero, handsome in his 90th year. He is standing in what is now a delightful flower garden, but which is where he was wounded in the spring of 1944.

It is where Slim besieged the Japanese and caused their general retreat. One of them wrote: "We had no ammunition, no food, no clothes, no guns. . . the men were barefoot and ragged and threw away everything except canes to help them walk. . . At Kohima we were starved and then crushed."

This devastating conclusion to the Japanese Burma invasion took place on a village tennis court. On Remembrance Sunday, the Colonel says the Kohima words, "For your Tomorrow we gave our Today." Slim's army reached the Chindwin that November. We sit on the sofa and turn the pages 62 years later. The river glints coldly through the fruit trees; the dogs have an armchair each. Then evensong.

On Monday, the winter in spring creeps away, and I am so happy that I forgive a badger or someone for gnawing the raspberry canes. The pear blossom is magnificent, and the plum blossom is pretty good.

A pheasant runs in a London Marathon-like way through the orchard, taking enormous bird-strides. My spade goes into the gorgeous old farm soil a treat. Straight-row digging is at this moment the best thing ever.

The rhubarb is showing. Everything is above ground. Everything is faintly warm. It is William Shakespeare's birthday — an April boy. It is over, the unseasonable time when "coughing drowns the parson's saw. . ."

Being Barak

Each near-dawn, tea in hand, cat on the make, I sit watching the great hazel filter in the day. Its companion was coppiced two years ago, but, remembering how this tree let in the light with a gradualness that suited me, I stayed my hand. What petty power, I now think. It shames me to write it down. But there it is, the 40-foot hazel with its frothing catkins and fanning boughs, and the small man coming to.

At first — it is 6.30 and still January — it does not more than shift darkness. But by seven it is a mutation of sumptuous verticals of colour. Then the sun fires it, and the uncurtained window is too blazing to contemplate.

Yesterday, something very odd occurred. Forty or so men trotted over the hill and into the valley. Backpacked, not chattering like the crocodiles of ramblers, they were soldiers getting up steam — maybe for Afghanistan. Easy on their feet, they passed through the hazel screen so quickly that I might have imagined them.

Later this morning, I listen to Thomas Tallis's mighty motet for 40 voices. It is a music that overrides religious division and paltry argument. What price bank scares, what price anything that leaves out the eternal? Like the radio presenter, I heard it in Blythburgh Church ages ago, the 40 voices waving and weaving their way to the painted angels, and out over the marshes. Having begun, they cannot end, at least in one's head, in one's devotions. How do the singers keep their places in this articulated glory?

Afterwards, dizzy with voices, I pick up fallen wood for the stove, and all the trees join in — although I am not so heavenly "sent" not to see what needs lopping. Wild daffodils, those that Dorothy Wordsworth noted, are in bud under the plum.

During the debate about having judges or kings, Jotham tells a delightful tale about the trees' arguing over who should be their monarch. It is in Judges 9. "The trees went forth on a time to anoint a king over them; and they said unto the olive tree [and to the fig, vine, and bramble], Reign thou over us." And, being wise, as all trees are, they made their leafy excuses. No fear! Trees have better things to do than to reign over each other. And so had many of the Shechemites, it seems. After telling his tale, "Jotham ran away," which is just like an author.

A noticeable thing, if I may say so, is how un-Bible-read the worshippers are these days. On Sunday, I preach on Barack Obama's namesake, that Hebrew hero who saved his nation and whom the writer of Hebrews links with David. "Arise, Barak, and lead" (Judges 5). Isn't this what they will have cried on Super Tuesday? He and a woman, Deborah, would rescue their country. So nothing is new.

Why do not so many of us read scripture for pleasure, or as a last resort on our desert island? Its stories are infinite; its poetry is enchanting. In it, the trees are enthroned and crowned as only nature can make them, and as they are in my old garden at this moment as the latest sap anoints them.

My lovely hazel (*Corylus avellana*) has high standing in the Christian universe; for did it not provide Dame Julian with her divine nut? A cock pheasant scuffles beneath it, kicking up black mould. "You need to coppice that tree," advises a passer-by. Do I?

Blythe's Corner

Early Ascension, early Pentecost, and early heatwave. Such a May! Rosy apple-blossom, Van Gogh rape, blue-green wheat, diving swallows, psychedelic bluebells, and a kind of lively warmth that is unlike that of a hot August, and which caresses one in the lanes.

The Queenslanders arrive to check up on our common forebears. All Australia, they say, is mad about a BBC programme, *Who Do You Think You Are?*, and tracing families on the internet is all the rage.

Terry has traced ours back to the 18th century — not there, but here in Suffolk. If he could have his life over again (he is at least 45) he would be a genealogist. He unloads his findings: a fat packet of Blythes, only a few known to me via family gossip, and most safely at rest in the births, marriages, and deaths registers until — in Queensland — Terry stirred their bones.

I am to take him where their dust lies. It is only just up the road — well, 12 miles. The sunshine polishes the hired car from Heathrow. The ladies on the back seat cry "Look, look!" as the yellow rape or a thatched house sizzles by.

I show them my birthplace, which was a thatched house until it burnt down just after the last war and is now a pair of neat bungalows. We glide on.

There is a shock — mine of delight, theirs of consternation — when we reach Blythe's corner in the churchyard, the resting spot of all those rustics on Terry's internet Domesday list; for, unlike most of the ancient graveyard, it is a waving meadow of cow parsley, bulldaisies, summer grasses, and lanky cowslips, the latter "paigles" to us. "Wildlife Area" says a card on a stick.

Through the wildlife, I can just see Uncle Fred's cross and Aunt Aggie's biscuit-coloured and shaped stone. Uncle Fred, who ploughed, fought on the Western Front, and fathered five children before he died at 25. Aunt Aggie, who gave us falls from her orchard, rubbing them on her skirt and showing us the bit that was safest to eat, a large old woman in a little house straight out of a picture-book.

Her house had a brick floor, an apple room, and a fire that never went out. Speckled photos of young soldiers hung on the walls, and polished brass shell-cases stood on the mantelpiece. The house was full of silence. When I last came to her grave, a sycamore tree was growing out of it.

The Queenslanders took many pictures with their digital camera. A gentleman seated by the church door was reading a book, *How Jesus the Jew Became a Christian*. I stood by the

Victorian font where I was baptised — the medieval one lay outside, split in two. A pair of marvellously dressed men lay on either side of sanctuary, Sir Robert de Bures in glorious armour and Mr Jennens in periwig and ruffles: one all in brass, the other all in marble.

And there, between them, the folk in the Wildlife Area sang Merbecke and hymns about rest. How they toiled! But less so in May. In May, there was comparatively little to do on a farm, except to feed stock. Suffolk sheep were still in the meadows, ancestors, like us, of a local breed. But the yellow rape, the thatch, the hired car slowed down before them.

John Betjeman takes the Train

The extent of Betjeman's radio career came as a bit of surprise. I knew that he loved being on television, though not out of conceit but from his delight in film crews, good natured young men who cheered him up and banished his melancholy. He was, too, quite a performer.

Now a friend has sent me a fat offering of his radio career, 50 of his pre-telly talks — and what a revelation! They show him as a writer growing up and yet at the same time, and typically, staying put, for this was his genius and his plight.

I met him once when he awarded me a prize for my *Guide to Aldeburgh Church*. This was in the crypt of a City church, with wine and smoked salmon laid under the memorials. He was convivial and kind. In one of his radio talks he apologises for his appearance, of all things, telling the listeners about his buck teeth, his yellow skin, his untidiness. In the crypt a kind of shambolic radiance made these things unnoticeable. On the "wireless", he was what he would always be, a pointer to past values and to future values.

The sound of his voice must have seemed rather reactionary, but, as we listened all those years ago, and usually to our discomfort, it began to sound prophetic and iconoclastic. In order to make the 20th century listen in the roar of its Modernism, he makes it look back at what it would willingly have abandoned, given a chance. Good things. Beautiful things, and, of course, unfashionable things.

During one of Betjeman's last broadcasts, fed up with being dubbed "nostalgic", he tells his listeners — they were multitudinous — how much he loathed this word, saying that it went with "nausea". He said that his aim was to revive a correct use of the word "sentiment". Good for him.

Many of the '30s broadcasts rage against Victorian values, and especially when it came to the subject of their "restoration of medieval churches, where they often did more damage than the Reformation". Then, gradually, persuasively, marvellously, Betjeman taught us, planners and ordinary folk alike, to appreciate the glories of the 19th century.

He became the singer of the "seaside", the railway stations, the suburbs. His "Oxford" voice directed us to his beloved Cornwall, where the golf club was given equal space to the coves and cliffs. The talks, though "light", are profound. Shown the fittings of a country church, we are shown a deep but uncertain faith such as we ourselves have.

Many of the talks are about the Second World War, about eccentrics, about friends, about the writers he has known, about solitary religious people, and about Anglican saints such as Isaac Watts, Augustus Toplady, William Barnes, Parson Hawker, and

Pugin. They open up to us the Talks Department of the BBC and we see Betjeman gradually moving from the bondage of the script to "free flow".

The radio became part of his economy as a writer, as it did with so many authors. It was a mark of having arrived to broadcast regularly. *Trains and Buttered Toast** I found a treat. What began as a formal chat would end as prophesy.

* *Trains and Buttered Toast*, edited by Stephen Gawes, John Murray.

Maytime

I preach on the Comforter, and when has he been more needed? Oh, the unique bereavement of all those Chinese parents, now that the earthquake has taken their one and only ewe-lamb! "O Comforter, draw near," we sing. What inspired Christ to christen his Spirit such? "I will not leave you comfortless." Rachel weeping for her children would not be comforted, however.

Now and then, here and there, the earth's surface cracks up, and our topless towers fall on us beautiful, delicate mortals, as we do our maths and revise our lessons. Or the typhoon rages through our estuaries so that their benign waters can wash us away. These huge tragedies are neatly slotted between the telly chefs and the football.

I remember a William Empson poem, "Aubade", which I put in my Second World War anthology: *Writing in a War*:

Hours before dawn we were
  woken by the quake.

My house was on a cliff. The
   thing could take
Bookloads off shelves, break
   bottles in a row.
Then the long pause and then
   the bigger shake.
It seemed the best thing to be up
   and go.

Go where? For the poet, the war was the earthquake. His youthful life of reading, drinks, girls, was shattered by it; so the best thing was to accept it. He is witty and philosophical. As for me, I give up trying to imagine the unimaginable, these vast disasters, the loss of so many only-children, and go out in the early evening to put anti-badger netting around the kitchen garden.

The late birds sing — a monotonous chiff-chaff, and a solitary white-throat. The badgers in their sandy sett could be watching. I sprinkle the runner beans using a fine rose. A cold wind rises. Whitsun, I think.

The Australian relations arrive, but have driven off to Stratford-upon-Avon. I miss them. They were so good. Terry, the driver, was enchanted by the cow-parsley lanes in which the cars passed with such civility. "No hassle!" His return waves gradually took on a quite Elizabethan flourish. The ladies on the back seat added their smiles. And now that East Anglia is over, it is on to Shakespeare, and Cornwall. Emails have been flying to and from Queensland. No one is really away from home these days. People get up and go, but never out of technology. Our weather meets their weather in seconds.

Meanwhile, back at the ranch, the Flower Festival looms in view; little boards all along the roads into the village proclaim its eminence. Although no judge of these things, I am told on good authority that the Wormingford Flower Festival is quite something. Visitors arrive from miles away. The flag flies on the Saxon tower, the Stour glints through the trees, the marquee bulges from its ropes, and the church is Chelseafied, and I tell myself that it is good for our souls, as well as the quota.

"You will miss the flower festival," I told the Australians. They looked puzzled. What with spidery, flower-blocked lanes, what with Gainsborough having walked them, the density of England is what they had not reckoned with. And I have never done with it; for who could? It is the May growth that retells each year. One should live to have many Maytimes, and to be comforted by them.

Our "Wickede Worme"

Stephen climbs on a chair to photograph the dragon-crocodile from whose jaws dangle the pretty bare legs of a Wormingford maiden. A First World War St George strides above this pitiful scene, and stares Stephen straight in the eye. I hold the chair.

The window is gloomy, but digital cameras dispel gloom, this being their function. Bright the vision that delighteth is what they have to do.

We are taking a picture for a postcard of our celebrated local legend. A knight returned from the Holy Land with a crocodile. It terrorised the parish, lived in the mere, and demanded girls for dinner — all this owing to the "Worm" in Wormingford, which we equated with John Wycliffe's name for the serpent — "Sith that wickide worme . . .".

The etymological truth that our village is named after Widermund who kept the ford cuts no ice here. All the same, I might ask Stephen to provoke the neighbours by making another postcard of Widermund's crossing. It is where Essex meets Suffolk, and kingfishers flash.

We had just returned from hearing the nightingales at Tiger Hill. There, among the grey-blue of acres of withered flowers, we listened to the wonderful overture of chook-chook-chook and the slow movement of piu-piu-piu which followed it, and felt immortal.

The guest gone, I fix more chicken-wire round the potato-bed in which a badger has been snouting, and try to think of something original to say when I preach at the Flower Festival. I think, too, about Alison Uttley, for whose *Diary* I have to write a foreword. The white cat sprawls on a willow, and thinks of human love.

At Phyllida's bookstall in the barn, I buy three Agatha Christies for Ian, a young man with a lust for old authors. Church bookstalls are dreadful witness to the unlovable nature of so much current literature, the white airport blocks, untouched as it were by human hand, pristine, dead. The politicians' memories and cookbooks, the grubby DIY manuals, the computerised fiction, the blockbusters that only burst the luggage.

But here is a nice paperback of Muriel Spark's *The Girls of Slender Means*, squashed between stacks of *Reader's Digests*. You will recall — I speak now to the joyous possessor of real novels — that these girls are members of the "May of Teck Club which exists for the Pecuniary Convenience and Social Protection of Ladies of Slender Means below the age of Thirty years, who are obliged to reside apart from their Families in order to follow an Occupation in London".

It is 1945, and, as the blurb says, the war is grinding to a halt. But not the youthful Muriel Spark. She is away! And still is, I discover, as I dip into her by the font.

On Sunday, the heavens opened. The sun hid. The track became a flowing road. The river was fretful, its surface rising into watery versions of a golf-course tee.

Dace and roach swam in its still depths, unmoved by the downpour.

I imagined the procession at Walsingham, the dark majesty of all those clerical umbrellas and the soaked skirts, and the Protestant Truth Society hurling its spears and getting wet. And, maybe, "What Christ's Mother sang in gladness, Let Christ's people sing the same." Old friends will be there, splashing along.

My procession is Bernard with the cross and Pip with a loyal voice. One of my feet squelches a bit.

The Bookshelf Cull

The last fairweather visitors gone, it suddenly occurred to me to change the books in the guestroom, no more than this.

I was recalling how the previous owner of my house, the artist Christine Nash, never changed the bedside offering. Year after year, as I lay there, at first under an oil-lamp named Globy, I would read and re-read Richard Hull's masterpiece *The Murder of my Aunt*, or *Cold Comfort Farm*, or ancient gardening catalogues, as some restless creature or other scuttled in the vine behind my head.

I once murmured to Christine, "Always the same books."

"Yes," she replied, "always the same books."

41

Now I know why. Should you carry a dozen volumes from one shelf to another, you will most likely be carrying hundreds before you finish. Sequences will be thrown out; titles will have to be regrouped; subjects will demand respect.

On Wednesday, we all had lunch at the great house, and were shown, of course, into the library, where a basket-grate blazed with logs, and the gilded spines in the tall bookcases glimmered, and a grand orderliness undisturbed for generations spoke critically to the readers of our day.

I would actually love to read in this tall room, love to mount the ladder and come down with, say, *The Army List* or the *Crockford* for 1887. But then the butler would show in M. Poirot.

Back at the farmhouse, there is no time for reading if the mighty business that began at the bedside table is to be concluded. First, a large box for the chuck-outs, the space-makers. Then, the mighty pause. What Christian hand could dispense with a 1901 history of the Quakers, spider and all? And might I not need four different editions of *Emma*?

Letters and reviews drop out. Long-borrowed volumes cry: "Thief!" They form a penitential pile, and will be returned to their own country. Here is the typewritten poem which that fine poet David Gascoyne gave me as we stood outside Marks & Spencer's one busy afternoon. It is called "Sentimental Colloquy".

The evening in the town
Summer's over
Has always this sadness, Conrad;
And when we walk together rain
As darkness gathers in the public gardens,

There is such hopelessness about the leaves
That now strewn in heaps along each side
Of the wet asphalt paths . . .

"Hear, hear," I say to this ghost; for below my window lies a private garden, where leaf-wise things are indeed pretty hopeless until the 12 oaks shed themselves, and this won't happen much before Christmas — which should give me time to do all the books.

Four shelves for the Letters, a whole wall for fiction, a swaying corner for poetry, a den for Lives, plenty of room for the obese.

On and on I go, staggering up and down stairs, cuddling to me the treasures and the once-read and the ten-times-read, the gifts, the nice pick-ups, the inheritances (including those old bedsiders), the ceaselessly bought, the rarely abandoned — which is why the cardboard box is only a quarter full.

Today, everything is held up because I am sitting on the floor reading Elizabeth Burton's *The Early Tudors at Home*, with the white cat's paw as a bookmark. Pages, leaves, dust, volumes of all three.

Taking Jenny Joseph to Wiston

It is exactly 50 years since we replaced the ancient church that the German bomb blew to dust, and Bishop John arrives to see what we have done in the mean time. Housekeeping-wise, a huge amount. But, while acknowledging this, he feels it his duty to draw our attention to the sacredness of the building — every church building.

There is a Herbertian severity, or shall we say seriousness, behind his kind words. The family silver is paraded on the altar, cups and dishes touched by all those generations of village people. Cold spring winds whip around the churchyard. Our priest, Henry, walks between the war-torn memorials.

I walk behind the Bishop and read from Paul's Letter to the Ephesians, the bit in which he writes gladly about a broken wall and a fresh architecture of which Jesus Christ is the cornerstone, and speaks knowledgeably about all the building being fitly framed together so that it can be a holy temple.

George Herbert loved the word "temple". His friend Nicholas Ferrar knew this, which is why he entitled the poems *The Temple*. Paul, of course, goes on to tell us that we are a temple within a temple, a sacred construction ourselves. With infinite tact, the Bishop draws us away from the housekeeping to the stillness within both us and this phoenix building.

Jenny Joseph ("Warning — When I Am an Old Woman I Shall Wear Purple") comes to lunch. But, although an old woman, she is wearing a nice tweed motoring cap and a capacious motoring coat. We have mushroom omelettes and rosé wine, and then we drive to the little Norman church to see St Francis preaching to the blackbirds.

Well! It is entirely filled with scaffolding. An intricate cat's cradle of steel pipes and platforms divides its interior from floor to ceiling. The scaffolders swing about happily. The dog-toothed arches feel youthful. Why, it is 1120 all over again. A church is going up in a field, men are going up ladders, benefactors are totting up the cost, a bishop of somewhere or other is standing in the wet grass, his crozier at the ready.

The bells are being cast in the graveyard so as not to run the risk of their getting cracked on the foundry cart. Mass is being said in a builder's yard. Hammering and lugging stops for some singing. *Aeterna Christi munera*, maybe. Trampled flowers (it is mid-May, of course) lift up their heads.

And now, a millennium later, the scaffolders are back; the buttercups are crushed; the old arches are grinding their dog-teeth because of the interruption. A young workman, powdered with Norman dust, hurries after us as we leave. We have left our umbrella, the special one that Jenny purchased at the special umbrella shop in London.

The painted apostles and angels will be blinking across the aisle in what for them will be their first experience of a cloud of unknowing. Shouldn't the workmen wear masks? The silver tubes give out little screams as they are screwed into place, and these follow us as we make for the gate.

The Rector will be saying her evening office in a neighbour-ing parish. Jenny drives on and on to Minchinhampton. I tell the white cat how fortunate she is to live in a house where spring-cleaning is a minimal event.

I must cut the grass so that the Flower Festival ladies do not carry my sloth into the wide world when they come for alliums and spectacular leaves.

A Farmer's Wife

The passing of the farmer's wife — for as long as any of us can remember, a distinctive voice in the land. The rain holds off. The church fills with farmers' wives from all over; farmers, too, of course. I walk slowly before Geraldine under the churchyard limes, in the telling silence that precedes the Sentences, and think of them, these robust countrywomen who used to do "the writing" and who still are an indispensable force in the management of a village.

Geraldine's life had been plain for all to see; for her farm adjoined the church, and her cows and other animals took part in Rogation. Her pretty grandchildren sing "Yea, though I walk in death's dark vale Yet will I feel none ill" in the front pew. And I talk about farmers' wives in general, a host of them making their no-nonsense motherly way through my head.

Barry tolls the bell, Tony reads what farmer John wants us to remember about his Geraldine, and then we sing, "O, that old rugged cross, so despised by the world, Has a wondrous attraction for me", the neglected hymn surging through the church and out to the stockyard. And then everybody gets into big cars and drives them down into the valley for the funeral feast at the inn where Constable's barges had a rest.

Farmers' wives have not been left out of agricultural history, but their role has been somewhat taken for granted — though not by Thomas Hardy and George Eliot. Emma Woodhouse, of course, doubted whether it would be possible for her to meet one.

I like Dorothy Hartley's account of them in her wonderful book *Lost Country Life* (Pantheon, 1979). I told the congregation about it in my funeral address. It was women as well as men who made the English landscape, and who decidedly made the English country garden.

The farm labour-force has gone, but during its generations of existence it was the farmer's wife who nurtured it, patched up its hurts, fed it, and bossed it about. Often of an evening in my ancient farmhouse, I think I hear the dairying, the bread-making, the calling, the singing, the never-ending toil. I hear the same bells and the same water-music from the stream. In the churchyard, the farmers have done their wives proud, and their names are spread out on handsome tombs.

Country deaths stir up a residual faith. It is not to be analysed, but accepted. We have to die in order to put on our immortality, I tell the understanding crowd.

The Psalmist was sad when he looked across the fields and realised that he was no more than a sojourner there, "as all our fathers were". He is rueful because his beauty is "consumed away, like as it were a moth fretting a garment".

And yet — I preach to this mourning, knowing assembly — farming people are lucky; for whether they followed the plough or now steer the combine, the marks they leave behind possess a certain indelible quality like no other on a local earth. This farmer's wife and her husband John were unaware how intensely "local" their lives were — how unlike even the lives of their farming neighbours. It endeared them to us.

I read them a poem by John Clare:

Love lives beyond the tomb,
And earth, which fades like dew!
I love the fond,
The faithful, and the true.

A Composer Arrives

Jonathan and his vast machine make their presence known as they return the overgrown track to its medieval highway, the one down which the brass knights in the church would have galloped. The noise is fearful: a grinding of boughs, a chewing of bracken, a screaming of greenery.

The machine leaves a piecrust edge to the lane. Jonathan comes in for his dues.

"I must pay you."

"Yes, you must pay me."

He has a fringe of Tudor-red hair and is also large. But how marvellous to be accessible to organists and churchwardens once more. How nice to saunter, instead of battle my way, to the top. The corn can be seen waving beyond lawn-like banks, the stream through the oaks. There is a sweet smell of crushed plants.

Peter-Paul Nash the composer then arrives, that silent walker who appears unannounced with a haversack of music on his back. Composers refer to whatever they are composing — symphony, sonata — as "a piece". It is etiquette not to enquire after the piece's progress. So he sits down and we have lunch on the step: Cheddar cheese, Ryvita, and Granny Smith apples. The white cat, purring only a little less proportionately noisy than Jonathan's Moloch, joins us.

And thus the summer day passes. Left on my own towards evening, I weed. Farm gardens are really nettle and horsetail forests through which roses and irises have to find their way. I pull up about a million weeds, listening to the night-song of the birds, and making up a sermon about Barnabas the Apostle en route, as it were.

Georgian parsons had sermon-walks where they could wander and think what to say for two hours each Sunday. Poor, poor labouring folk, having to listen to this after weeding the cornfields by hand. I shall talk of Barnabas the consoler for ten minutes. But, I tell him, I do love you, Joses from Cyprus, with your soothing nickname. And we will assure him:

> Distant lands with one acclaim
> Tell the honour of your name.

My new book buzzes in my head all through the weeding, all through Jonathan's mighty crunching, and partly through lunch. Peter-Paul will under no circumstance ask me, "How is the new book going?" Its pregnancy is apparent, but private.

Long ago, I did have a friend who would follow me up hill and down dale, telling me the plot of his new novel, and "What did I think?" and it was very dreadful. Hush, let the unborn story make its way without a spoken word.

A favourite joke of mine — I may be repeating it — is of Dumas rushing from his study to tell his wife, "I have finished *The Count of Monte Cristo!*" And her saying, "But dinner won't be ready for another hour." So he went back to his desk and began *The Black Tulip*.

I had a teacher who would create uproar in class with such jokes and who would then shout, "Settle down! Settle down!" Which was unreasonable.

The dentist tells me tales about his son as the stopping hardens. He is good at this. He tells me about Durham University, and the sharp bend in the River Wear, and I would like to tell him about standing by Cuthbert's tomb with my month-old godson in my arms, but I am gagged. How kind he is, giving me such a nice smile at my age. Think of the merciless teeth of Jonathan's hedger!

Love Entire

Here I am, far from home (one mile), battling against the winter, as I walk to the archaeologists' dig. I am observed from little hot rooms. "Poor old chap. They shouldn't have pulled down the workhouse."

Hailstones ping-pong against my face. Half the sky is black, the other gold. I take shelter in the post-office shop with Marcia, and Gerald the shop dog, buy stamps and frozen peas, and decide against the dig.

Another Tuesday. I think of the great lodge on its hilltop, battered for centuries by weather like this, but for ages lying snug beneath the grass; and of the multitude of huntsmen, including Elizabeth I, who ran to it for cover on days like this.

Halfway home, the air grows still. Blowsy daffs wave to me. Birds become operatic. House-builders creep from cover. Somebody puts the washing out.

Somebody has sent me Peter Carey's lucid account of his Buddhism. It floods me with light, and I would pin it up in the study, only I find that I never quite "see" what I pin up. Better to read it thrice and so contain it.

Carey had a Baptist missionary ancestor who said: "Expect great things from God; attempt great things for God." But what captures my full attention, being at this moment in a situation not dissimilar to his, is his quietly confident: "No one dies. During the past seven years I have lost my wife, my mother, and my son, as well as two marvellous older friends. Of course there is huge sadness, but in the eye of eternity where can people go? Nowhere. They remain an intrinsic part of who we are. Bodies are temporary: love survives."

The poetic Christian geography of the afterlife cannot

survive in a scientifically understood universe. Christ taught the immortality of love. I find that people are more haunted by the possibility that they will not "know" those they loved best than by "heaven" or "hell". Asked one of the trick questions that so often came his way, Jesus replied that "In the resurrection they neither marry nor are given in marriage." In other words, earthly relationships are transformed there.

When I take a village funeral, I stop the undertaker's sergeant-major's "All stand!" I want the rustle of the procession at the ancient door and my "I am the resurrection and the life" to suggest an entrance to Love entire. All that we can do at death is to "survive" like the Lord. Like Peter Carey.

Tony Venison comes to lunch, or I actually take us to the Nayland pub. No three-hour winter now, but a return to the spring-in-winter warmth, the delicate Thomasina crocuses prinking (Thomas Hardy) the lawns, and the hellebores fit for him to inspect.

For many years, he was the great gardening editor of *Country Life*, and we all, plants and humans, have to sit up when he arrives. I carry out his instructions to the letter. And plant his gifts. And we sit in the old once-bargees' inn by the Stour with the river firing our beer.

There are some people who have just been to a country house to see its owners, but Tony has just been to see their catalpa or their dying rose. "Welcome, welcome!" they cry as his little car noses up the grand drive. Back at the farmhouse, he touches a leaf as a doctor feels a pulse, shakes his head, and says: "I should replace it, but not in the same spot."

With Vikram at Bemerton

I doubt whether George Herbert knew that Bemerton means "the place of the trumpeters"; or even whether the Royal School of Church Music, in nearby Salisbury Close, is conscious of those glorious fanfares by the Nadder.

Maybe the trumpeters were made to practise well away from Old Sarum, so as not to disturb its peace — or, rather, the singing of the Sarum rite, which would eventually flow out to cathedrals and parish churches to this day.

Herbert remains Anglicanism's most musical voice. Izaak Walton said that he was tall and straight, lean to an extremity, very cheerful, and "a very good hand on the lute, and set his own lyrics or sacred songs". So imagine Mr Herbert at his Mattins. The Sunday before he died — the windows tuberculosis-wide — he got out of bed, tuned his lute, and sang his final song. He would have been in good voice, I imagine, as his music joined that of the trumpeters.

Much later, and in another room, my friend Vikram Seth would add to the continuous music of Bemerton. I have built up a little base there quite haphazardly. It began with my walk-book *Divine Landscapes*, when I was wandering towards the cathedral for the first time, and the Bishop caught us up — I was with my walk companion, Alan — and drove us into an already packed building.

It was the annual service for the Wiltshire Mothers' Union; so we sang "Jerusalem", and then crossed the meadows to Bemerton. And there it was, the little church, the big rectory —

though no Vikram for a long time. And no Judy Rees, no Michael Mayne, and no Timothy Dudley-Smith; for all these people were waiting in the wings. But gradually they emerged to play their part in my life.

My contribution was to edit George Herbert's severe *A Priest to the Temple*. When I came to the signing session, Judy Rees had brought Herbert's cup from its glass case for me to use. It was one of those tall, Elizabethan vases in which the wine lies low.

This Advent morning, the sun shining on my holly hedge, I search for music in *A Priest to the Temple* for the sake of this piece. Goodness, he's strict! When will he lay down his strictures and pick up his lute? Never in these pages. The only mention of music is as a metaphor for rectory behaviour, "So that in the house of those that are skill'd in Musick, all are Musicians, so in the house of a Preacher, all are Preachers." Not only the parson, but also his family and servants, are to witness to Christ.

There is no musical instrument in Herbert's inventory of church fittings. Yet there he was, lanky and ill, and singing to his lute for all to witness, his Christ listening, and the Bemerton wind in what remained of his lungs. And the lovely words brimming with gratitude.

Today, among the Christmas cards, comes what we must all have longed for, an extension of those five or so Herbert hymns that for so long have been all that we could sing of his poetry. It is called *Another Music: Through the year with George Herbert*, and it is published by the Friends of Bemerton Church and the Royal School of Church Music.

Now we can sing, as he did, not only "Teach me, my God and King", but (amazingly), "The Pulley", Barry Ferguson's setting of "Easter", Alec Roth's "The Flower", and, for this week, "Christmas", in which Herbert's voice joins that of the shepherds and all the Christmas singing since.

Ten more newly set Herbert poems for the hymnal. What a gift. I will give them to Meriel to play.

With Judy at Bemerton

A quarter of a century ago, Alan and I "walked" George Herbert for a book I was making about divine landscapes.

Never could I have imagined re-walking this route with Vikram Seth. But so it is. Our maps joined when he purchased Bemerton Rectory.

> I heard it was for sale and thought
>   I'd go
> To see the old house where
> He lived three years, and died.
>   How could I know
> Its stones, its trees, its air,
> The stream, the small church, the
>   dark rain would say:
> "You've come, you've seen, now
>   stay."

Thus, after the poetry reading, we gather in Herbert's sloping garden: myself, the neighbours, the pilgrims, and Vikram's family, the light failing, the birds calling. And not for the first time.

Vikram — a kind of non-religious Hindu-Anglican, his priestly Buddhist brother, their parents, and my dear host Canon Judy Rees (Welsh) have been united, as has everyone else, by a village parson whose language has become our sacred lingua franca.

"Another poet in my parish?" Herbert asked. "From India? did you say?"

"Indeed", replied Vikram.

Joy came, and grief, love came,
    and loss; Three years —
Tiles down; moles up, draught;
    flood.
Though far in time and faith, I
    share his tears,
His hearth, his ground, his mind;
Yet my host stands just out of
    mind and sight,
That I may sit and write.

In the afternoon, Judy Rees had taken me on a long walk to Broken Bridges and beyond. Wheat and barley ears were just emerging from their green sheaths. Waters collided noisily where the medieval mill had stood. Vast silver birches toppled above blackberry thickets. Wiltshire chalk surfaced in the shape of flints. A woman passed, shouting into her phone. Oh, leave it at home when you come this way!

There were signs of floods, of feet, of contemplation, of weed-killer round the edges, of passage. This cornfield, I thought, is identical to that which I left behind at Bottengoms Farm. The Nadder, too, current-wise, keeps time with the Stour.

We spoke of Herbert's sickness, which he said "was working like a mole within him". And I remembered a niece who was at this very moment experiencing this painful tunnelling. TB would bring him down, so that he could rise up to his Friend.

At breakfast, instead of grace, we read his "Mattins". His was a quiet strict voice, one made beautiful for his listener, Christ. Oh, the frightful row he has to hear sometimes when we, his followers, get together! "Turn it off, for pity's sake, when you walk my path."

There was a luncheon party in an early Victorian house with a Raj-like veranda. Then we sat in a circle round the piano to learn a fifth Herbert hymn to be added to those in the book. "How fresh, O Lord, how sweet and clear are thy returns. . . ." Coleridge loved this poem particularly — called it "delicious".

A Singing Quiet

After dinner, I telephone aged friends, trusting that I will not be interrupting their gruesome TV — wards through which hefty nurses stomp up and down, police stations where the sexes collide.

"No, I was just dozing." This old friend is 92. "Oh, yes, I sleep well, and in the daytime, too!" Laughter. So what she hopes for is not "rest", but a great awakening.

I watch Stephen Hawking spell out Big Bang or something like that, being more or less illiterate in his science. The screen sparkles with space and time, all of it brilliantly suggested by a man who can scarcely blink. Well, I think, God himself was worn out by his creativity and, amazingly, had to take a rest.

It was on this admission that the writer of Hebrews constructed his beautiful concept of Christian rest. Tired out with life's toil, we enter the rest that Christ offers. Hence that somewhat automatic statement on the tombstone: "At rest". What shall we put? Put what is usually put, at rest.

In the recent experience of the farm labourer, miner, slave, factory hand, servant, death was "rest". In our experience, it is the uncomforting conclusion to the long rest we call retirement.

Victorian hymns are often frank and accusative. Vast numbers of singers, especially those who were getting on a bit, ached all over on the sabbath — and where would they have been if God himself had not taken a break? Working, working. For centuries, employers — the majority of them, anyway — would not have dared to break the third commandment. There was a kind of weekly holiday, and its social benefit was incalculable. Stroll through the City of London, still, on a Sunday — and the bliss!

There are two sets of the Ten Commandments, one in Exodus, one in Deuteronomy. It is the Exodus set that gives a religious reason for keeping the sabbath, and the Deuteronomy set that gives a humanitarian reason for not working that day. But both extol rest. Scriptural rest reflects the Middle East and its historic wanderings.

There are "resting places" which remind me of those of our East Anglian Gypsies, with their short-stay marks: a hearth, beaten grass, litter. And there are efforts to get away from milling crowds, those which are now as familiar to us as football supporters.

Once, having endured their uproar, Jesus told his disciples: "Come ye apart and rest awhile." And once, having walked all the way from Galilee to Samaria, he rested on Jacob's well. It was early morning, and it was far from resting time for the woman with her water jar. The weary Christ was often allowed to rest in the Bethany house or by the roadside, or to fall asleep in a fishing-boat. Rest was allowed him — that otherwise restless figure. And we rest in him — "Rest in the Lord", as the psalmist advised.

Unless I am sound asleep, I seem to rest in activity, if this is not a paradox. Doing — reading, particularly — is my refreshment. But, taking the service, I "do" the minimum, and hope that my stillness will activate prayer.

I love the singing quietness, the daydreams during lessons, the observed order, the faces of the country people, the outside cry, the clunking clock, the resting neighbours below the windy trees, the sacred vitality and both the brevity and the everlastingness of everything.

Soon the congregation will be resting from Sunday dinner under the Sunday papers, and I will be resting with a space. "I should have lain still and been quiet" — Job.

John Whale Dies

So, A second Railway Age dawns. New tracks are to be laid, and the glorious superstructure of the first will no longer be endangered by ignorant politicians. What havoc they wrought in their day — though mercifully not to our viaduct.

John and I were talking about it, he having lived in its shadow for most of his life. It came into sight, so to speak, when we were discussing the habitats of nightingales, how they loved blackberry thickets, and John said that there were dense ones at Chappel in the rail cuttings.

Chappel is where Mr Bruff and Mr Wythes built the viaduct over the River Colne in 1847-49. First of all, they thought of using timber, but they settled for bricks, all of them made locally. Eighty feet high, 1136 feet (346 metres) long, it straddles the pretty river, and takes our breath away.

John's great-grandfather helped build it, walking miles to the site, along with an army of brickies. The scaffolding hardly bears thinking about. Ropes and dizzy planks. Swaying cat-walks in high winds. Clinging figures. People fell off. Viaducts cost blood as well as money.

The line that the Irish navvies (navigators) laid across Rannoch Moor was expensive in hurt and death. It was floated on bracken beds. John and I put down our glasses (it was breathing time after Songs of Praise) and remembered how poor men once toiled — where our stunning viaduct was concerned, not unlike Pharoah's brickies. And now, if they are lucky, the commuters can arrive home to the sound of nightingales.

My dear friend John Whale, who invented this column, has gone to his rest. We met when the *Church Times* was printed in Colchester, and he would drive down, calling at Bottengoms en route.

There would be wonderful letters from Villers-sur-Mer in Normandy in his elegant hand. His Anglicanism responded to mine, creating a bond. Writers have to have a few real letters a month, a year — from writers. John's were such.

We met through a friend when I was chairing a committee whose task it was to choose the best religious radio and television programmes for an award. But we really "met" in our letters. He was a great man. All these different meetings.

It is Midsummer Day. Thinly veiled blue sky, a southern

wind. Loud robins. A rattle-trap machine of sorts is crashing about behind the hedge. All the windows are wide. Convolvulus winds between the kitchen bricks. I lie in the garden, reading the letters of W. H. Auden, and the white cat lies on me. No one would believe how hard we are working. Papers blow about.

Auden's inherited high-churchmanship runs like one of those clear rills that one moment are open to the heavens and next are a concealed movement. Like so many of the major poets of his day, he climbs from university stage to university stage, making a pittance. They said that at home he would sit at his desk from nine to cocktail time, whether he wrote or not. He is a Christian whom many of today's Christians should read — to be startled, shocked even, but eventually to be better-informed.

The massive volume dents the grass. Ladies call for "the list" of July sidesmen and lesson-readers, and we have mugs of tea. July for Deuteronomy and Matthew. How well the apostle would have known this majestic book. Its name means "repetition of the law". The Jews know it by its opening phrase, "These are the words . . .".

The Ante-room

It is six-something on a summer's morning, and I am lying on my back listening to *Something Understood*. The north window is wide to Suffolk, and the east window is wide to Duncan's hayfield. The bedroom is enormous by today's standards, and smells of wax polish, ancient dust, linen, old books, and the double philadelphus that looks in. What is being understood on the radio is death and life, in that order.

Of course, there is no understanding of such a progression without recourse to poets and composers and visionaries generally. Thus I hear for the never-too-often time Charles Causley's "Eden Rock", in which his youthful parents and his far-from-youthful self look across a Cornish stream at the pre-death, pre-life moment. No Bunyan river, frightening and hazardous, no trumpets blaring on the other side. Just the sound of a 'Twenties picnic.

Charles's father died soon after the First World War, but his mother lived on to a great age. He cared for her after teaching all day, and often wrote his poems in her room. She was an invalid, and not the pretty girl smiling at him across the stream. I would add, "And love to your Mother," when I wrote to him.

Carers were minimal. Charles did it all. And when she at last died he was bereft — which astonished his friends; for what a happy release! People do not understand the varieties of human love and their intensities.

Anyway, I am lying on my back in a room in which babies cried, lovers slept, and quite young folk drew their last breath for centuries, and am thinking what to say at matins. Now they are playing Messiaen; now speaking the mystic language of St John the Divine. All the poets, composers, and philosophers agree that where the death-into-life business is concerned, words and notes fail them. Yet somebody has to express the inexpressible.

Charles Causley, to my mind, does it best. At the *Songs of Praise*, rambling from hymn to hymn in the flower-filled church, I reached Sabine Baring-Gould, and all owing to Charles. We were on one of his mystery tours, and there at our feet in Lew Trenchard graveyard stretched the author of "Now the day is over".

To equal this surprise, I guided Charles to Edward FitzGerald's tomb at Boulge, replete with roses from that of Omar Khayyám in Iran. It was midnight and also Charles's birthday. The car glittered in the moonlight. We could see to read the inscription, "It is He that hath made us and not we ourselves". He was, after all, a very odd person — the poet, not his Maker.

On Thursday, I sat with a dying friend. A run of Dick Francis novels above his head, the not discomforting whiff of old tobacco. The garden at the door. The tea on the tray. The dog whipping the furniture with her joyous tail.

There is a moment when we pass, not only beyond the concerns of our day, but into that not unblissful ante-room to what we begin to see but cannot describe.

Writers have made a good stab at it, the subject being irresistible, often grandly like Milton, rarely as simply and convincingly as Charles Causley. Most of them have conflated the rivers, Styx, Lethe, Jordan, etc., which bear us away into scarifying floods, but his "Eden Rock" returns them to a bright, hurrying little stream in north Cornwall — the kind one can leap across.

Two Pilgrimages

The entire village school is setting off on pilgrimage from the Tabard Inn, aka The Crown, as I write.

I should be with them, but have pleaded mortal sickness, having already pilgrimaged to the shrine of John Clare on

Saturday, the altar of Mount Bures on Sunday, and to dear Bill's funeral at Dedham on Monday. Somebody had to stay at home to write the books. But what a fib, when I am as strong as a horse.

I excuse it by reminding myself of all the virtuous things I have done concerning the pilgrimage: lent the children my best tambourine and thumbstick, a costume last worn by Paul Nash, and much excellent historical information.

Two holy priests, Henry of Wormingford and Kit of Wiston, will bless them on the way. There will be bread and water at Tom's farm, a toll to cross the river bridge, pennants, a tall cross, and frequent singing. This is one way of getting these boys and girls out of cars and computer dens.

I have composed a Franciscan prayer for them, and maybe I shall catch their song as they wind through the cornfields, all 20 of them, plus ten grown-ups. They have raided the vestry for cassocks and done their Chaucer homework. Who will be the Pardoner? Who the Wife of Bath?

They should have knelt before St Francis Preaching to the Birds in Wiston Church, but it is full of scaffolders. So it will have to be Mr Storey's barn, a sacred enough place.

"When, nature prompting their instincts, small birds who sleep through the night with one eye open make their music — then people long to go on pilgrimages, and pious wanderers to visit strange lands and far-off shrines in different countries. In England especially they come from every shire's end to Canterbury. . ."

It was cold and hot by turn when we went to Helpston to pay our annual homage to John Clare. We went to Maxey Mill, where the boy poet was sent by the landlady of the Blue Bell Inn to fetch flour, since it was a few pennies cheaper there. He was slight and fearful of the fenny will-o'-the-wisps. Flour is very heavy, like concrete before it is mixed. He lugged it along the dead-straight road.

Maxey Mill is made of Barnack stone, and has wooden shutters and ladders. Dust falls from it endlessly. We left it to visit Mrs Clare's grave, where her great-grandchild Dorothy laid a handful of flowers.

Staring through the bus windows we saw Clare's Northborough house, the one in which he was so unhappy, as it was all of three miles from his birthplace. It was for sale for more than half a million, and had trim lawns and a fine garage. And we paused briefly to just make out the grave in Glinton churchyard of the woman who became his muse, the now legendary Mary Joyce, who was burned to death.

"What distinguished Clare is an unspectacular joy and a love for the inexorable one-thing-after-the-otherness of the world," said Seamus Heaney. And thus home, via the alternating borders of Cambridgeshire, Huntingdonshire, Suffolk, and Essex, the car flashing below vast containers, and the harvest glowing in the late sun.

And so to Dedham, and Bill, once member of the General Synod, once our treasurer, and always one of those laymen who hold the Church together one way or another, and whose life is a pilgrimage without their knowing it. "A lot of work" is what he used to say when I told him what I had been up to.

New Testament Ladies

A hot and, so far, sunless day. The high-up planes from Stansted must be getting the blaze. I fill the watering can from the stream and sprinkle the geraniums, the parsley cushions, and the runner-beans. There is desultory birdsong.

I work on the proofs of a new book, edging my ruler from line to line, looking up untrustworthy spellings in the dictionary. A publisher once said, thinking to do me a favour, "We'll do the proof-reading for you," imagining my relief. But I replied, "No fear!" I haven't written a whole book to be done out of its nice drudgery. Thus the hours pass, getting hotter and hotter, and the windows wide, and the uninspired birds calling in the wood.

Since it was the feast of St Mary Magdalen on Tuesday, I took her into the octave on Sunday, and preached on "The Women in the Lord's Life" to about 20 folk, including a singing baby.

I tell them that it was Phoebe who carried Paul's letter to the Romans. This is the letter that concludes with the first roll-call of Christian women. The roll-call begins with "Phoebe, a fellow Christian who holds office in the congregation at Cenchrea . . . stand by her in any business in which she may need your help," and then goes on to include Mary, Tryphena and Tryphona, Julia, Nereus's sister, and what sounds like a hard-working male-female Church on its first legs.

Just in case we all get carried away with Pauline equality, however, there soon appears the apostle's exact teaching to Bishop Timothy: "A woman must be a learner, listening quietly with due submission. I do not permit a woman to be a teacher . . . she should be quiet." But that was then.

I am sure that if Paul were here now he would be glad that our dear Archdeacon Annette isn't "quiet", or my friend Canon Judy at Bemerton. But maybe he was thinking of Bishop Proudie's wife.

Mary of Magdala — not a respectable woman, some said — stood her ground with the other ladies to watch the appalling execution, and would have the first human encounter with the resurrected Christ. Not one of the Twelve, but the brave girl from the seaside village who (some said) had touched him with scandal. But it would not have been because of this that he now murmured, "Do not touch me." Together in the early-morning garden they announced, as it were, the quiet birth of the Church.

The Jesus who liberated women from "devils" or instincts and behaviours that were out of control was the wise leader who set them free from all kinds of male restrictions. Nearly all his radical answers to women's questions were brought about by chance encounters. His ministry was peripatetic. He was a Saviour who was always on the move.

The easy access that they had to him created gossip. One woman told him to his face, "No man ever spoke to me like this before." And who provided him, the weary walker on earth, with a safe house? Those listening-cooking sisters. He was the one who gave women with a past a future, and women in the present an equal opportunity with men. Paul could not go this far, but he named many of the women who helped to bring the Church out of little Palestine into the vast Roman world.

I hope that the holy woman at the well — precursor of the Wife of Bath? — lived long enough to see it. Who ever heard of such a thing — a Samaritan and a Jew drinking from the same cup?

Carl and Philip, Electricians

Rain sweeps across the corn in silvery-grey sheets. The harvest has start-stopped, and the combines have crept back into their lairs like nervous dragons. Then the sun comes out, as blatant as you like.

Then Carl and Phil arrive with a great splash of electrics; for the deed is done, or soon will be. The farmhouse is to be rewired. They look without comment at the fuse-box, a museum piece. Then they ascend to the loft, a vast space straight out of Gormenghast. I dreaded this. I thought that it would fill the rewirers with horror and scorn. On the contrary, they are young, and they wander about in the beamy dust with wonder and grins.

But when they descend, Phil is pale. They have found a wasps' nest, and he is terrified of wasps. The nest actually belongs to my hornets, who have lived up there since William and Mary. Only I don't tell Phil this.

Carl is a gardener, is 29, and plays *boules*. "Everybody plays *boules* where I live." He is waiting for an allotment. "Only, sad to say, a holder must pass away before I get one." I cut him some bamboo rods.

They work quietly and neatly from top to bottom of the house. Fearful wires and switches are pulled out, and state-of-the-art ones are set in. At elevenses, we have coffee and talk about the housing ladder; at four o'clock, we have tea, and talk about the weekend. Carl reckons that a Saturday night costs him £125, what with a drink or two, the dancing, and the taxi home.

They work like artists on the ancient cat's cradle of my

electrics. I look into their world. It is good and true and gifted. When Carl comes into the study, he says, "A typewriter! You don't often hear one of them." He listens as one would to a wind-up gramophone. He has cobwebs in his hair. By Friday, it will all have been done, the rewiring, the fearless switches, the new points. And to think that I was born by candlelight.

On Sunday, I preached on Memory. "Remember me when you come into your kingdom." "Do this in remembrance of me." What I actually talked about was not forgetting. I remembered Paul telling the Ephesians to remember that Christ brought them to life. His difficulty — horror, even — was the inescapable memory of who he had been.

I remember a bad painting of the Sea of Galilee which I fantasised about during Sunday school. The ships in the picture would sail to romantic ports and out of the frame. Nothing could prevent their voyagings. On the wall of the little Norman church down the river the ship with the striped sail on the south wall is art. Medieval boys would have daydreamed it sailing off the plaster into the Stour and then into the ocean. It is the common experience to have, running side by side, religious conventions and personal religious imaginings. They make us what we are.

We sing Psalm 97. "There is sprung up a light for the righteous . . . for such as are true-hearted." I announce the Farm Walk, the Bicycle Ride, the new postcard of the St George and the Dragon window. Anything else? As I have a farm walk every day, I will probably scythe the orchard and swipe down the seeding nettles and horsetail.

I say farewell to Carl and Phil and hail to their work. Now I can say "safe as houses" without a qualm. Room after old room is bright with their efficiency. The hornets go back to sleep. The ship on the landing can sail to wherever it was the artist Francis Unwin had in mind.

Little Gidding

To Little Gidding with Margaret, my fifth pilgrimage maybe. But who is counting? Left of the roaring A14 lies another route. The climate is breezy and grey, the landscape wide and empty. We hurry to catch a glimpse of Leighton Bromswold, George Herbert's prebendal masterpiece, only to find it locked. Oh, the shame of it. And more shame still as I am on my way to talk about his severe *A Priest to the Temple*.

> What church is this? Christ's Church. Who builded it?
> Master George Herbert. Who assisted it?
> Many assist who I may not say,
> So much contention might arise that way.

In order to comprehend Leighton Bromswold we must read "Church-monuments", "Church-floore, -porch, -musick" — and particularly "Church-lock and key". No one is quite sure whether Herbert saw his lovely gift to this place. He told his schoolfriend Nicholas Ferrar to make the building of it his "chiefest" care of all the responsibilities which he would leave him. Izaak Walton wrote: "Being for the workmanship a costly mosaic, for the form an exact cross, and for the decency and beauty I am assured it is the most remarkable parish church that this nation affords." And so it is in its way.

But now to Little Gidding and its essence of Anglicanism, its ancient hospitality and old friends, its many-layered welcome. Unlike the classic front a few yards away, I had never entered Ferrar House before, and never in a thousand years could I have imagined it to be full to the brim with so many people dear to me. After tea we set off to look at an elm plantation. The general notion that elms have gone forever requires amendment. These Little Gidding elms are thin and tall and somewhat hugger-mugger, but living elms they are. So we stand and stare at them as their topmost branches rock a little in the sky.

On the way back to the house I tell Vikram Seth about the vast elm near my house, well three miles distant, which defied the plague and has become an example of what this tree looks like to those who would otherwise have to search for it in a book.

We now all troop to Evensong in the darkening chapel, entering Eliot's "husk of meaning" to sing *Laudate Domino*. He came here on a May day in 1936 and knelt "Where prayer has been valid".

Past tense then, present tense at this moment in August. It all hung around in his head until the Blitz shook it out. The great poem emerges from bomb dust and the centuries of dust which obscured the achievement of the Ferrars. Burning London ignites Pentecostal truths.

> The dove descending breaks the air
> With flame of incandescent terror
> Of which the tongues declare
> The one discharge from sin and error,
> The only hope, or else despair
> Lies in the choice of pyre or pyre —
> To be redeemed from fire by fire.

I see Nicholas Ferrar, the fat bundle of Mr Herbert's poems in his bag, galloping off to Buck, the Cambridge printer.

"What title, sir?"

"'*The Temple*', of course!"

Gordon's Last Party

Northerly winds rage above and the sound is Wagnerian. Oaks and ashes clash, clouds race, rain flurries, and summer flowers take a thrashing. Now and then, having put on my gardening rags, I venture forth to renew my wall-scraping, these having lost all definition. The white cat watches from her favourite throne, the ancient stone sink in which generations of farm children were scrubbed. I can hear their protest above the tempest.

Tomorrow — Aldeburgh! Will the uproar last? I half-hope that it will. Already I can hear its mighty slap on the shingle and see its hurling darkness. I am going to Britten's old house where, ages ago, I walked with him in the garden. There were walls there, high and protective, above which the coastal gales raged.

How does one listen to the radio without hearing all this news? It is a problem. Now, they even hang *Thought for the Day* on a news item, so I try not to listen to that. Unless, of course, it is a Sikh thought or a Rabbi Blue thought. And further footling grumbles. Why do TV newscasters straddle? The only worthwhile straddler is Evan Davies, whose gleeful conveyance of dreadful economics is a treat. There he stands, rocking and grinning away, every figure to hand. It is almost worth having one's bank balance take a dip.

Presenters may have to watch the thin line which exists between youthful informality and vulgarity. Summing up the wonderful Elgar concert at the Proms, Aled Jones cries: "Not bad for the son of a piano-tuner!" But enough of this quibbling. There are Victorias to pick and branches to sweep from lawns.

We all go to Gordon's party. It is a highlight of the Wormingford season. The field has been harvested to make a car park. The garden has been weeded. Henry, the Vicar, has raised his beautiful tent which, clearly, has come straight from the Field of the Cloth of Gold. It billows fretfully and inhospitably, for the Northerlies are no respecter of garden parties.

Thus we crowd the farmhouse itself, and are cheerful whilst intermittent showers rattle the conservatory glass like lover's pebbles against a bedroom window. Talking to Tom about his herd of Lincolns, I find myself remembering Parson Woodforde sending his "saucy" man Scurle to Norwich to gather some news and bring it back to the rectory, and of the yearly Tithe party when — well, I had better not say what happened during this great spree. It was the eighteenth century, after all.

The *Ipomoea* which Richard Mabey gave me — sent in a wet parcel through the post — doles out its Morning Glory a flower or two at a time. Its name means "similar to bindweed". There are hundreds of species of it. Mine has bright purple flowers which bloom and wither in a day.

There is a kind of infallible succession of them, and their credo is clearly "less is more". They climb a bamboo stick by the front door, but unambitiously, staring beautifully out east and not up at the rose giddily waving above them. Their huge cousins trumpet along the track and wind themselves up in the telegraph wires, and make mats in the ditch, and are altogether glorious in themselves, though you would have to preach a sermon to make the neighbours admit it. In hedge-bindweed's case, less is obviously not more. Although nothing can be whiter than white, it makes a good try. Children used to love it.

Muntjac Calls

Dusk is the time to see friends. The day's heat is skeined across the corn, and the evening is still no more than a wisp of dullness against the blue. But it is at this moment that the muntjac appears in silhouette on the track, alert yet nonchalant, giving me his best side.

How different the following morning! He crashes out of the ditch, nearly knocking me over, and barking like all get out. "It is I, your nocturnal friend, your admirer. Calm down!" No use. The barking muntjac rises high in the air before disappearing, then reappearing in Duncan's corn all the way out of sight.

He — the muntjac — is a beautiful little Asian deer with maybe a Javanese name. Now and then I listen to him barking at the summer moon, and frightening the trees.

I meet Duncan and, after we talk acreages, he asks me to say "an agricultural grace" at his 80th-birthday lunch. I tell him that I intend to put a sign out, "Graces, Eulogies, Blessings to order". Back home I tell the white cat how good they all are to me, these farming neighbours who carry the collection to the altar, singing without the book, and who return my bow with due solemnity.

I dig up three rows of potatoes. How plenteous they look on the larder-bricks with their crumbs of earth scenting the cold room. Then St James, Son of Thunder, leaps from the calendar, as does his ambitious-for-him mother. I happen to be reading *Alice Through the Looking-Glass* when this lady requests the best seats in heaven for her boys; so I know all about the upside-down nature of things, the first being last, the master waiting on the servant, etc. Jesus is so perfect with her. The seating arrangements are not in his hands.

Then along comes a little king, Herod Agrippa, to kill poor young James. Small men in power do not put up with Sons of Thunder. And that should have been that. But, centuries later, James takes a lesson from the far-travelling fishes that often escaped his nets, and makes a silvery bid for Compostela, where, they say, you will find him to this very day.

Even if you cannot quite believe this, the long walk to him will do you good. I see him at high table in heaven, young and boisterous, and making up for an early death, and wearing a cockleshell.

The church doors are wide to the weekend walkers. They frame the heat. The cars in the lane will soon be ready to cook in. The ringers in the back row voice their favourite hymn, "To those who fall, how kind thou art! How good to those who seek!"

An odd thing occurred. Returning to the house and pouring some Islay whisky that a rich Cambridge professor brought me, and picking up *Alice*, I came to: "So they walked on together through the wood, Alice with her arm clasped lovingly round the soft neck of the Fawn, till they came out into another field, and there the Fawn gave a sudden bound into the air, and shook itself from Alice's arm."

"'I'm a Fawn!' it cried out in a voice of delight. 'And, dear me! You're a human child!' A sudden look of alarm came into its beautiful brown eyes, and in another moment it had darted away at full speed."

But no barking. Muntjacs were still in Java. Mine is full of airs and graces, having escaped from Woburn Park, and was on its way to the College of Heralds when it leaped into my vision.

Markings

They are laying Alexander Solzhenitsyn to rest in a monastery as I write, and I think of him, and of his two deportations: one to the Gulag Archipelago, the other to the West. His ingratitude for the second banishment amazed us. The West's vulgarity and consumerism appalled him. It was as though a Desert Father had been found a nice home in Las Vegas. He will be lying unlidded amid the sumptuous singing.

In *Cancer Ward*, he wrote: "Nowadays we don't think much of a man's love for an animal: we laugh at people who are attached to cats. But if we stop loving animals, aren't we bound to stop loving humans, too?" Last evening I watched two deer put-down on a venison farm. I also saw my barking muntjac dancing around Jean's horses.

Yesterday afternoon, I suddenly remembered some un-planted daffodil bulbs in the larder, and found a place for them by the stream. It wasn't so much raining as damping, the trees dripping, the air filled with soft wet flurries. Some cucumber seeds followed. I was now warmly soaked. But how pleasant it was to be out.

I marked willow logs for sawing, and a forest of nettles for their comeuppance. The contract man in his combine who had been cutting the first rings of harvest gave up, and there was a sudden silence.

I had walked all round this huge field last week, and had heard it sizzle with dryness. Now all is moist. Bees rock in the tender boat-shaped Balsam flowers whose resurrection name is *Impatiens noli-tangere* — Touch-me-not. Because if you do, my seed will leap into the universe. This beautiful water-plant has shot all the way from a Shropshire riverbank to the Stour Valley since 1632. And everywhere else besides.

The post-lady brings me news of *A Cropmark Landscape in Three Dimensions*, i.e. a report on what lies beneath the onions and sugar-beet, unseen until aerial photography. Barrow cemeteries, concentric ring ditches, long mortuary enclosures, and cursus monuments, some of them in Wormingford. Indeed, a line of them wall off a loop of the river.

Intensive cultivation to its meandering banks — to their very edge these days, with the price of agricultural land going sky-high — has become the single biggest risk to our Neolithic and Bronze-Age farmers' scene. I sometimes take my Christmas Day walk through these invisible sites that one must go heavenward to see, and sometimes carrying the thrilling photographs. The camera can look inside you, and, outside, can see humanity's timeless scratchings on the significance of death.

Thus to evensong for six, the rain-smirched light looking for the altar through the lancet of the infant Saxon tower, and Barry holding the hymns together, and the prayer felt. Now and then I worry about this monthly service. Is it minimal? Is it "all", as Julian would say?

Well, tonight it is everything. Forget numbers: think of validity. I read Isaiah. "And the glory of the Lord shall be revealed, and all flesh shall see it together." We half-dozen, and the ring-makers down by the Stour, and the Reverend Mr Cox, and the saintly Solzhenitsyn, and George Herbert, and Gordon the churchwarden.

The Great Essex Earthquake

The earthquake woke me up just sufficiently for me to feel the ancient house dip a fraction, then recover its oaken equilibrium. It was as though its beams were boughs once more and bending to a pre-Reformation gale. An oak had to be centuries old before it could be part of a new house.

For ages, earthquakes were believed to be the fury of God or the gods, nobody having an inkling of plates shifting. It took prophets ages to realise that God was not in the earthquake, but in the silence.

We had a tremendous earthquake all round here in 1884. It was on 22 April at 22 minutes past nine in the morning. People were hard at work. It was a lovely spring day. Mercifully, Mr Damant the photographer was about to record it. Quite a lot of folk were at matins in Sudbury, Suffolk.

At Colchester railway station, Mr Blatch was personally seeing his first-class passengers into their seats as they set off for the City. Just opposite, a workman was high up on a scaffold as he inscribed "Eastern Counties Asylum for Idiots" on a building. At Wivenhoe, Mr Stebbing the grocer was piling up tins of lobster, and Lord Alfred Paget was being rowed out to his yacht the St Cecilia. At Wivenhoe Hall, young Jackson was still in his bath.

And then it happened, the Great Essex Earthquake. No deaths

— but the property! How it fell to pieces! A thousand roofs slid to the ground; 20 churches were in ruins. Three entire villages went to wreckage.

Boats were thrown from the harbours on to the shore. There was a noise that nobody would ever forget. There was a blinding dust, and there was the pathos of what would later be the exposed interior, the wallpapered rooms hanging in the air, the fires blazing in the suspended grates, the unmade bed.

In all, 1213 buildings were half-demolished and there were splinters, splinters everywhere.

The famous Rose Inn at Peldon was made unsafe for smugglers, and the coastal churches, Langenhoe especially, were heaps of pulpits, ceramics, memorials, screens, etc.

Mr Damant hurried around with his fine plate camera. One of my favourite photos is his elegantly grouped picture of the Rector of Langenhoe and his friends standing in the ruins of his church clasping umbrellas and gently smiling.

They had curiously prophetic expressions, which would appear again and again during the next century, shaken looks that hid the shock, the automatic grin. And the strange stench of fallen architecture. All this would repeat itself — all over the world. And human beings would stand and stare at the swift demolition of their achievements as the dust settled, and would look so differently from how they felt.

On Saturday, the central heating gave up, and the farmhouse assumed its patchy warmth. Although I read the Instruction Book for all I was worth, there was no rush of oil, no oomph and flare. So the young mechanics arrived soon to emerge with faces of delight. What did I think?

"No, tell me."

Triumphantly: "A spider!"

The poor creature had crawled into the oomph-pipe and there it lodged, stopping the flow.

"It committed hara-kiri," said the boy mechanic.

"Can I see it — the spider?"

They shook their heads sadly. It had done its worst and was no more. Or maybe its best.

First Base

Christopher and I are driving slowly along the narrow, straight road that links Thorpeness to Aldeburgh, so that I can show him where I became a writer.

Thorpeness is an Edwardian fantasy that was created around an ancient fishing village just before the First World War, which became a favourite spot for Empire families to spend their precious "furloughs" from India and other pink countries. My bungalow predated the furlough village, and yet had clearly been based on one of those Raj retreats in the Hills, designed for use when the sun became too hot in the plains. It has a big sealed verandah facing the North Sea. Here I wrote my first book, a novel.

We can just make the bungalow out. The sea at this moment is a bright gun-metal grey. It flings up white spray. Flurries of rain hit the windscreen and Maggi Hambling's steel shells with their pierced words from Peter Grimes. There would be late-summer plants on the shingle, but we do not get out.

Further along, at Aldeburgh, a strip of coralline deposit runs above the shingle to form the Crag Path. It was while we were walking here that Benjamin Britten told me that he was "to go in for an operation". I stopped in my disbelief, but he tapped his heart.

And now Christopher and I, having glimpsed my bungalow, make our way to the Red House, where I haven't been since I sat in the garden with Ben and Peter and Imogen what now seems like aeons past. We are to celebrate the latest of the Aldeburgh Studies in Music, a book called *Imogen Holst*, and I see her, not here in the tall house by the golf course, but in her flat over the shop in the High Street, with its windows fore and aft, the gulls wailing on the sills, and the at-the-time inexcludable Aldeburgh draughts. There we would sit at her father's wide desk, putting the *Programme Book* together.

At the Red House, a dozen or so of us are shown around. Lots of paintings and drawings. Ben's desk with a polished stool, on which he balanced as he worked. The shiny pianos. His death-bed with its red coverlet. Our friend Bishop Leslie Brown was often beside it. Downstairs was Mrs Hudson's kitchen. Although severely Suffolk, her name and her power never failed to remind me of that other indomitable presence in Baker Street. I can hear Ben telling me: "Go to Blythburgh and ask the Vicar if we can hold a concert in his lovely church, Ronnie."

Carrying Imo's biography, which I long to read before getting home, Christopher and I travel to Snape Maltings to stare across the marsh. The rain has ceased, and the reeds rustle and whisper, the night birds call, the concert-goers' cars fall into their slots. The vast Victorian agricultural complex is slowly becoming a kind of arts parish.

Newson Garrett, who was the very epitome of the post-Industrial Revolution magnate, would, like God, have found it very good. This was his empire, and, in a sense, it still is. When I was a boy, the farm workers walked in bands here after bringing in their local harvest to earn some Christmas money at "the malt". The sweet scent of it wafted across the river. At the water's edge, the Garrett lighters bobbed against their moorings, waiting to take the malt to London, plus a few passengers who preferred a sail to the train.

And now about a thousand of us quieten down to listen to the Mahler Chamber Orchestra play Mozart's *Piano Concerto No. 13 in C*. And I think I see a thin, crinkly-haired figure in the wings.

In Defence of Mr Brontë

Three drones provide their August music all day, the combine, the grain-dryer, and the south wind in the poplars. The latter often rises to a roar and is sumptuous. It is as if the village is in full sail. The harvest is snatched between heavy showers. The Big Field was cut all night. Moonlight led the way. I lay in bed and listened to the solitary harvester as he grabbed the damp corn.

"What a difference!" said Susan the following afternoon. On her parents' Irish farm, and this only 40 years ago, harvest meant feeding the 5000 — well, a lot of workers — and it was making sandwiches and tea for 20 all day. This morning, the same figure in the lurching cab is lightly harrowing the stubble. No aftermath. No following birds. No shout of triumph. Only Duncan's dryer playing its part in the drone trio.

When Christopher and I went to Snape for the Mozart, Britten, Schubert concert, it was cool and still, the reed-beds hardly moving. They levelled off to Iken and Aldeburgh, the rivulets glittering round their roots. We sat in front of one of those people who come to concerts to clap, stamp, and bawl. How guilty one feels when one decides to end applause. The concert was good, familiar, and a pleasure to be at, and I would have liked its final moments to ring in my ears.

Richard Dawkins and Charles Darwin on television. Dawkins's evangelical atheism fills his face with a light similar to that of a saint. Which will not please him. Darwin is beetle-browed, his eyes filled with the suffering caused by infant death, as one by one his beloved children slipped into what he believed was oblivion, and what Mrs Darwin believed was heaven.

He and Dawkins come together in their tribute to the earth-worm. All that I can think of as the programme ends, and Darwin's battered leather armchair and Dawkins's bright face flicker from sight, and for no logical reason, is George Herbert walking along the Broken Bridges footpath with Jesus.

Having summed up the courage to call the electricians in to rewire the whole house, and the job done, I walk through the rooms, bursting with self-congratulation.

I miss Radio 1, of course, but my admiration for those who are able to trace faults through plaster and wood, much as a surgeon is able to bypass blocked veins, grows at every step. Nice new switches, nice new fuse box. I hear Carl calling from the loft about the dead rat. And Philip unable to take another step because of a live spider. Life is all arrivals and departures, I tell the white cat.

A Shadow Cabinet columnist in The Times dismisses Dudley Green's *Letters of the Reverend Patrick Brontë* in much the same fashion as George II dismissed Gibbon's *Decline and Fall of the Roman Empire* for being too thick.

Other than being the father of three brilliant novelists, Patrick

Brontë was a great curate. Mrs Gaskell left us with a caricature of this caring man. His writings show a very different person: a priest in a rough parish who fought for his people. Those who see the Church of England in the usual superficial terms should read this book.

Mr Brontë was never more than a curate, but then he never had to be. His Christianity was lived, and that was enough.

Blackberrying at Southwold

I was trying to remember when I first came here, as Vicki steered us through the holiday traffic. It would have been when little houses on South Green cost £400 and were not called The Bolt Hole.

The North Sea is a steady azure until it is within sight of the horizon, when it turns to skimmed-milk blue. The day is fair. The cannon point towards the invaders. The visitors are semi-dressed in pretty clothes, and there are some fine dogs. How delicious it is to be here after the A12 crawl. How could George Orwell have detested it? We park the car in a meadow, and go in search of Ian and Joachim, who are, we trust, cooking.

Southwold is having one of its white and gold "Nelson" days, with whipping flags and well-scrubbed humanity, and the white lighthouse standing idle. I imagine English Impressionist girls crowding the bridge and holding on to their hats. After lunch in the harbourmaster's cottage, we wander across the common and pick each other the first blackberries. The public benches are deserted, as everyone is on the beach.

"See that house?" says Ian. "It was built for retired servants."

Authorship has taken a hold every few steps. See that house? It is where Agnes Strickland and her sister Elizabeth, whose name never appears, wrote *The Lives of the Queens of England*. I look her up. "Her somewhat flat writings were extremely popular, perhaps because of their use in teaching." I see these Victorian ladies putting down their pens for an hour for a gusty stroll to Walberswick, their maid banking up the fire for their return.

There is a kind of concealed strenuousness about the Suffolk coast. Maybe it was about keeping warm — not to mention solvent. Or possibly it was the wind perking one up. But a lot got done — although at this Bank Holiday moment, nothing whatever is being done, and the ambulating sloth, the prostrate bodies, the faint calls create a lovely watercolour rest. It is as though the Mayor of Southwold has appeared in all her golden glory at a window and decreed, "Do nothing!"

Naturally, there are shrieks when a brave soul enters the sea, although Ian does so without a cry. But then he comes from Norfolk. Mostly, people sit outside pubs, deep in conversation. I thought that I would like to sit in an ocean-fronting window for a week, turning the pages of a novel, looking up, looking out, with a good cat for company. But the evening comes, and the Bank Holiday ends, and a few homing gulls wail their way along the River Blyth, and Vicki says, "Wouldn't it be nice to live here! What do you think?" It is a question we all ask after a day out.

Meanwhile, back at the ranch, the grass needs cutting, and the white cat needs adoration. And something has to be said at matins next Sunday, Trinity 15. St Paul is in Corinth, staying with some fellow tentmakers, a man and his wife. They were Jews who had been driven out of Rome by the Emperor Claudius, and, having suffered for their faith, they were in no mood to change it for that being preached by their lodger, no matter that he belonged to their trade. Eventually, all three of them sailed away to Ephesus.

What would have been happening on the Suffolk coast then? Well, the sea would have been baring its claws to scratch at the land, and no one would have been swimming, that's for sure.

Strangely Orthodox:
R. S. Thomas and the Poetry

The work of R. S. Thomas has been deeply explored, but more by literary critics than by priests. Now we have two Welsh archbishops, one a considerable poet himself, taking a profound glance at him. In his foreword, Rowan Williams sees him as a great writer "on the edge of the Christian tradition"; and for Barry Morgan he is someone who has done much to form him spiritually since he was a divinity student.

Dr Morgan and Thomas met at the very end of the poet's life, and Morgan, then his archdeacon, took his funeral. Eventually this little but great book emerged from some quiet-day talks given at Tymawr Convent in Monmouth.

So much has been said about Thomas's uncomfortable — and uncomforting, on the whole — God, not to mention the poet's often scary personality, that these aspects of him have obscured what he really believed and who he really was. In a few clearly written pages, Dr Morgan disperses this popular cloud, and lets us see who created some of the best Christian poetry in existence.

R. S. Thomas stirred it up: the beautiful bland worship, the very presence of God in it, the question of what Jesus actually said, the kindly easiness of much religion. Non-religious critics have found satisfaction in what they think is his fundamental non-belief, and have praised his courage as well as his genius.

Dr Morgan's is not a defence of the Church's position, but gives a wonderful short and eloquent essay on the depth of Thomas's faith, its profundity and grandeur. His mentor was Søren Kierkegaard, and if we begin there we shall know where we are. Thomas's metaphor was birds, and, if we look up at them, we will enter his vision. His guide through priesthood was George Herbert, and "The Church Porch" was framed in the hallway:

When once thy foot enters the
Church, be bare. God is more
there than thou; for thou art
there only by his permission.

Thomas defined religion as the response of the whole person to reality, and poetry as the imaginative presentation of it. What has disturbed us in the past, before we came to comprehend him, was the imaginative reality of his truths.

Dealing with his — to many, at the time, rather shocking — confession of an absentee God at the altar itself, Dr Morgan reminds us of the beseeching cries of the Psalmist, and the anger of Job. Mankind was ever finding God missing where he should have been most present.

R. S. Thomas found a unique language in which, first, to discomfort the Christian, then to set him on his corrected way.

Has not each of us, kneeling in church, saying the great words, felt nothing, seen nothing, and then experienced the following?

> I would
> have refrained long since
> but that peering once
> through my locked fingers
> I thought I had detected
> the movement of a curtain.

Thomas's honed worship and acceptance has a bleakness beyond, or outside, that of historic Puritanism. When he says:

> We have over-furnished
> Our faith, our churches
> Are as limousines in the
>   procession
> Towards heaven . . .

we worry a bit about the central heating. He was a Herbertian for whom, in today's philosophical jargon, less was more. He never celebrated facing the people; he was indifferent to hierarchy; and was frequently furious. Hugely admired in the world of literature, he should have been greatly misunderstood at home. But with accounts of his belief, such as this one by Dr Morgan, we discover that all the doubt and "awkwardness" which we pile on to him are really still ours.

He said what we at times dared not to think — a 20th-century Cuthbert. "Birds are migrant creatures and so come and go, likewise God." In the avalanche of religious publications, the Christian should discover this small book.

Becoming Old

We have two evensongs, one every Sunday at Little Horkesley, one each month at Wormingford, one with the biggest attendance, one with the smallest, and both stemming from traditions that are largely forgotten.

Churchgoing rules and figures in the countryside were created more by the timing of the main meal on the sabbath than by its prayer pattern. To enable their army of servants to have time off for God, the middle classes had dinner at two instead of eight. They went to matins (and holy communion about four times a year), and their staff, having washed up, laid the table for supper and, dressed up, went to evensong.

There was much singing and, afterwards, long walks, then home again strictly by ten. And, of course, it was preeminently the service for the farmworkers and their families. Usually the best television of the week, plus, I used to suspect, some connivance by the clergy to rid themselves of this service, has resulted in the actual oddity of evensong in many minds.

It is, of course, liturgically most beautiful and spiritually entirely satisfying. Just to read it at home at about four o'clock sets the day right. If our three churches were nearer, I would read it in one of them, but they are miles away. So, I sing it alternately with Henry, the Vicar at Little Horkesley, along with this surprising-to-some large attendance; and every first Sunday in the month here at Wormingford, with the Colonel, the bell-ringers, and the churchwardens, the two candles wavering, the four hymns, too.

And I think to myself how good I am at Quiet control. Not even the wild goings-on of Jonah disturb us, or the lukewarm antics of Laodicea. All is submerged in ancient prayer. But for sermon I read both the great and small evensong folk something I have written about the sea-routes of the early faith, and I think I imagine its sound like the entrancing noise in a shell when it is clasped to the ear and entirely listened to.

To Norwich to talk to the annual general meeting of Age Concern. It is convened in one of those hotels that have conference suites, and I am met with a stand which says, "How to arrange your funeral". We are far from evensong.

In my late 40s, I began to write a book about old age, feeling Time pressing on me. It was a philosophical riposte to Simone de Beauvoir's brilliant Marxist tirade against the dying of the light, and also a kind of stand against some of the ideas that have created today's old-age management.

An old lady was telling someone, "And when she saw me she said, 'Why, you keep on looking younger!'" But what an incomparably better world it is for the old, with its dentistry, hygiene, pretty clothes, disposable income — and long, long years. Four-score-years-and-ten are becoming the norm. Christ raised only the young from their death, those like the governor's daughter, or the widow's son, or his friend Lazarus, who deserved a life to live, not those who had already lived it.

And so to King Street in Norwich, the city's first entrance, by the side of which a very old woman went on living long after she had written a book called her *Revelations of Divine Love*. She said that "We need love, longing and pity," curious necessities, some now would think. When she was 30, she thought it "a pity to die"; so she got better in order to be a writer, among other things.

The Seedsman's Celebration

It is getting on for six, and still I lie abed, automatically listening to Farming Today. I feel that it is my duty to report any cheerfulness that might break into its professional misery.

This morning, the programme tells me how the rain has caused the combines to get stuck in the mud. Well, I want to retort, are there not still thousands of people alive who harvested with their feet stuck in it? The Prophet Muhammad prayed: "O God, make it rain round us, and not on us."

The pastoral imagery of the world's religions is most in evidence at this time of the year. Heard, but not felt, not seen. Machinery alone bears the pain and gains the glory.

The dual depression caused by the puddled field, Bunyan's Slough of Despond, which squelched away both yield and joy, is virtually unknown to the present harvester. I see them on my Victorian tithe map, those sinks in the soil which the binder skirted if it had any sense. Theologically, they represented the ups and downs of village life, though never its *De Profundis*. One would have to plunge far deeper to experience this.

Tess was en-route to this godforsaken void when Thomas Hardy demoted her from the lush pastures to take a turn at trimming swedes.

> How it rained
> When we worked at Flintcomb-Ash
> And could not stand upon the hill
> Trimming swedes for the slicing-mill,
> The wet washed through us — plash, plash, plash!
> How it rained!

After breakfast, clad in my thistledown-light waterproof and wellies, I walked to the depressions on the tithe map. The combine had scooped the corn out of them, and the harrow had combed them into shiny ridges. I thought of the soaking plough-horses being geed round their perimeter, and the ploughman with wet sacking up to his thighs, and the little indented pond glinting evilly.

As John the seedman and his wife, Sheila, are 50 years wed, we join them at the golf-club restaurant to celebrate. Their 1958 wedding album invites our glance. How can people be half a century younger and yet just the same?

The electronic equipment thumps out the "Anniversary Waltz", and they dance. In the photograph, they smile in front of the church porch, c. the Armada. Guests take to the floor and hop about. Grace has been said. We eat rather a lot. We feel a unity of spirit. The golf club has grown out of the strawberry fields; the strawberry fields out of the aerodrome; the aerodrome out of the cornfields; and all in a lifetime.

Through the broad window, I watch a watery sunset, the runny colours, the blackening of the day. I think of a trip round the great seed-sheds with John, and listening to his amazing facts.

He has been, all his working life, custodian of our seed temple. A million million separate entities of plant existence were there in the dust and dusk, just waiting. To think that Paul and John Nash painted their Western Front pictures in a seed shed.

I give the Golden Weddingers a book, and they say, "We will read it in the winter."

Mostly Apples

The line between hedonism and contemplation can be pretty thin. Here am I, watching the mists unveil the hills, one by one, toast in hand, cat on lap, when Donovan makes an unlikely entrance on the Today programme to preach Transcendental Meditation.

The years fade, and I am sitting on Aldeburgh beach while friends, hot-foot from the Maharishi, attempt to convert me to bliss. Switching over, I hear viol music by William Lawes, he who composed "Gather ye rosebuds while ye may", and who was killed at the siege of Chester, aged 43, leaving behind much bliss for posterity.

At five to eight exactly, the sun jumps into view like a smartly flicked coin. I devour one of the marvellous old apples that David brought me from Crapes Fruit Farm, and think of another day, also long ago, when Sue Clifford and Angela King came to see me.

They were to launch a venture called Common Ground. What did I think? Common Ground would inspire, inform, and involve us all in learning about, enjoying, and taking responsibility for our own bit of natural history, be it in town or village.

A few years later, now trusted savants of Britain's ecology, Sue and Angela proclaimed the crunchy feast of Apple Day, and not a moment too soon; for our orchards had almost gone, and our stores were piled high with waxed and tasteless stuff from over the water.

When you enter the supermarket, think of England! Confound it with your cries for not only Richard Cox's Orange Pippin and Blenheims, but Beauty of Kent, Dutch Codlins, and Worcester Pearmains. All apples descend from the genus Malus, a word that also doubles for bad, thus causing confusion in Eden.

Adam and Eve eat "fruit", not an apple. "Comfort me with apples," says the Song of Solomon. "Go and see if there are any D'arcy Spice on the old tree," my friend John Nash would say. These ancient apples would sit on the sideboard until they were wrinkled enough to face the Stilton and port.

Leaves rain down and pheasants stalk the grass in their lordly fashion, heads bobbing, gorgeous tails dragging. I have to do the honours for the Apostles Simon and Jude. Like the apple, Simon is described by a word that means two things, Canaanite and Zealot. Jude, of course, never has a day's peace in the modern Church, having to find what we lose.

It is thought that they died together in Persia. I love Jude's wonderful commendation: "Now unto him that is able to keep you from falling, and to present you faultless before the presence of his glory with exceeding joy, to the only wise God our Saviour, be glory and majesty, dominion and power, both now and ever."

But he can be fierce. "Clouds [we can be] without water, carried about by winds; trees whose fruit withereth, without fruit, twice dead, plucked up by the roots. . ." Like our apple orchards. And then there are "murmurers and complainers". Nothing changes. I shall go to Andrew Tann's blissful apple orchard at Aldham, and see its harvest, smell its infinite variety, and buy its diversity for a pound. No sprays, no boring skin perfection, but here and there a blackbird's peck and something pleasantly out of the round.

Let me not be a cloud without water, a fruit twice dead. Andrew's apples lay denominationally in separate wooden realms of deliciousness, keepers and eaters awaiting their moment.

The Burial of Lt. Rupert Brooke on Skyros

OUTSIDE, the rain-clouds race; inside, the papers strew the room. Half a shelf of books has given up all propriety and lies like abandoned ethics all over the study floor.

In the ordinary way, I would have returned Rupert Brooke to his niche as a poet one has done with in Eng. Lit. What a curse those old reading lists were, with their chosen essentials, their "requirements". So I read what I clearly have never read before: Brooke's "Success". What is he saying? And that John Donne-touched poem "Dust"...

The thin black volume continued to spread its mottled pages, and suddenly I thought of a pub in my Suffolk home town, and myself about 18, discussing Rupert Brooke with another boy, and a little fat man joining in with: "I helped to dig his grave." It was the Ind Coope brewery traveller.

Then he had been a rating on his way to the Dardanelles. An officer was taken ill with blood-poisoning. Maybe a mosquito. The officer was tremendously famous as a patriot poet, it seemed. Within hours he died, and there was consternation. The ship put in at Skyros, and a burial party was ordered to dig a grave. The ground was rocky, and he and the other sailors found it tough going. It would be the ground that would be "for ever England".

I wish that it was possible for me to remember more of this conversation; that I had asked this or that. I do know that on later visits to the little pub, seeing the brewer's traveller in his usual corner, I had enquired, "Did the Captain or the Chaplain read, 'O spare me a little, that I may recover my strength before I go hence, and be no more seen'?"

On another ship that was also on its way to the Dardanelles was my father, George, aged 17. Rupert Brooke was buried on 23 April, St George's Day. Shakespeare's birthday, too. He told his friend Eddy Marsh that "the word 'England' seemed to flash like a line of foam." It was 1915.

Stephen arrives, and we walk in the Woodland Trust fields, now sprouting oaks and almighty trees. The River Colne wetlands have really taken off. Juicy grasses, myriad flowers, leaping deer, delectable air, smoky-gold water, Colchester turned to Athens in the distance, and the relentless roar of home-bound commuters all too near.

As I am Patron of this particular Woodland Trust site, I swank a bit. Stephen, immensely courageous, enters blackberry thickets with bare legs. I hang over the bridge and try to make out a perch, a pike. House martins ride the air thermals, as do gliders from the old bomber base. We find a plastic boomerang, which gives me the opportunity to tell Stephen one of my favourite jokes.

"Do you know what happened to the Aborigine who bought himself a new boomerang? He couldn't get rid of the old one."

What a long time we have lived. Several Brooke times. There are dragonflies on the River Colne and on us, but so un-wounding, so bright. His watery meander was the Cam, of course. Which could be pretty stingy. But we had to wait for that poison, the Aegean cup. He was all of 28.

"You have been reading Rupert Brooke?" asks the incredu-lous voice on the telephone, making it sound like something one should have got over a long time ago. But there are lines that one cannot get over, I discover.

The Rule of St Edmund

I awake at dawn to find someone sharing my bed. A bat. He lies still on the sheet. Could he be one of the bats for whom at great expense the parish has provided social housing in the south-aisle roof? I enquire. He says nothing.

I try a more eloquent question. Does he realise that the day will come when a man will cast silver and gold idols to the moles and bats?

He says, "What on earth will I do with them?" So I place him tenderly in a cup, and carry him through the drenched grass to an ancient shed and leave him to his bat thoughts. Then the white cat and I return to the kitchen to dry our toes.

On Thursday, a young Turk drives me to St Edmundsbury Cathedral. We discuss the virtues of the local towns. He and his wife do not care for Colchester, but it is good for mascara. They love Bury. They picnic in the Abbey garden. She is only part-Turkish and has blue eyes, he tells me enthusiastically. He failed his first driving test in Bury, but it wasn't Bury's fault.

I am early for the Chapter meeting because of his speedy progress, and walk through the morning streets expecting canons to the right of me and canons to the left of me. But they are all in the Cathedral drinking coffee.

Bury smells of bread, like Chartres. The sun polishes Edmund's flinty name on the new tower. Dean Neil hands out our Rule, and thank goodness; for anything might happen in a College of Canons without a Rule. It contains the Edmund prayer:

Christ Jesus, with the life and martyrdom of St Edmund, King of East Anglia, you inspired generations of pilgrims in the way of love and hope. Enfold your Church in the mystery of your life, that we, in our own pilgrimage, may be apostles of your wounded and risen glory. . .

After the eucharist, the Dean and I stare over the wall into the fragments of the vast Abbey. "Where do you think he is?" The bones and dust of a 29-year-old. That target for the arrows. In the cosmos. Pensioners nod on municipal benches, children shout in the dorter enough to wake the dead. Home on the bus.

"No more return fares," says the driver.

"Never?"

"Never."

In Norfolk, my friend Ian Collins gets Sister Wendy to open his art exhibition in the airy Salthouse church. She arrives in a taxi, is of course inimitable, but is soon rather anxious about the time. Ian thinks that it may be time for her Rule, but it is actually time for Sister Wendy's Wimbledon, she knowing that there is time for everything under the sun.

I, too, watch the great drama. It is played out to perfection and at length, and is hugely civilised. Nadal looks like a descendant of Matthew Arnold's dark Iberian who, on the Cornish beach, "undid his corded bales".

But the big question is, "Shall I dig up the potatoes, or leave them another week?" Their bloom has gone; the stalks (hulms) writhe in faded strings. But any day now the fork will go in, and the smooth spuds will surface. It is a moment to live for. I will let them lie in the light.

Saxons Ploughing

It is not quite warm enough to sit outside, although here I am, reluctant to admit this. The afternoon sun appears five minutes each hour. There is no wind, just an October stillness trapped and waiting. Ash leaves sail down like perished hands. Bells ring, although from what direction it is hard to say, the river being in one of its oblique moods and carrying sounds from confused directions.

Peter-Paul the composer is on his way. The mysterious satchel will be riding on his shoulders. Sustenance for a three-mile tramp? The latest score? I must not ask. He will be passing Wiston Mill, passing Garnons, looking about him as he does. The homeward commuters are fuming on the A12 but as yet I do not know this, living as I do in another world. A gas tanker — leaky, they think — blocks their weary way.

The white cat teeters along a wall, piteously calling for food — anything will do — smoked salmon, cream; heaven knows that it never asks for much in exchange for being so beautiful. I finish reviewing new books about trees for the TLS, adding up the words and fixing the pages together.

Peter-Paul appears. He has a satchel on his back and big clumping shoes. He has been surprised by a heron and grati-fied by a buzzard. I give him cake and tea. He can't sit on the garden chair because it has collapsed; so he squats on the doorstep and talks about music in novels, rather disapprov-ingly. "Why do they do it, these fiction writers, tell stories about musicians when music itself is rather beyond them?"

I say that the characters in a quartet or a quintet, or an entire orchestra, if it comes to that, offer the novelist an enclosed group on which to work. Think of The Archers, I nearly add, but think better of it.

The first novel about music I ever read — in my teens — was *Maurice Guest* by the Australian writer Henry Handel Richard-son, who was a woman. It was about a love affair at the Leipzig

Music Academy. Suddenly remembering it, my heart stands still, as they say, and I have a huge longing to read it all over again. Is it in the house? Unfortunately, Peter-Paul has left before I can stun him with this wonderful tale. Next time.

Gordon the churchwarden arrives to collect thankful items for Harvest Festival. I supply baking pears and honey, plus the usual instructions that he, great servant of Christ, does not need. Have I any time? No. Should I turn some of my Discoed-Presteigne lecture on ploughing into a Harvest sermon? Why not?

I imagine the Wormingford fields being ploughed with Saxon bullocks, the poor animals plunging up and down our hills, the ploughmen, their legs cross-gartered, singing lost songs. Or simply swearing, the share splitting the amaranthine flints. The latter now and then edge their way up in the track, sharp as razors.

And — now I am in a fanciful mood — I see a Roman from Colchester, half a dozen miles south, and not cooped up in his wall, taking a nice walk on what was once my land, and seeing what I see: the swerve and dip of it, the unchanged contours of it, the same nip in the autumn air of it, and, of course, the pencillings made by the plough across it. And in his temple a thankful pile of sheaves to Ceres from it. His Celtic predecessors went further. They put an ear of corn on their pennies.

So now to the thankful pulpit.

Enthronement

To Bury St Edmunds on the streaming bus for the enthronement of our new Bishop, a young man from the North.

The new tower of the Cathedral shines in the rain. Gorgeously attired folk new to us, or at least to me, take their places.

Soon, after many a wise word and a banging on the west doors, the Bishop from the North is led to his throne, a soaring piece of tabernacle work into which his golden person fits perfectly.

There is an immense assembly of old Suffolk friends, and much music. Britten, of course. The Bishop's left hand and right hand are anointed, and we sing, "Hast thou not seen All that is needful hath been," which is indeed the case. My robes are not now quite as damp from processing in the drizzle. Everything in sight is very beautiful. Tiny boys sing plainsong:

Sacerdos et Pontifex et virtutum
    opifex,
pastor bone in populo, sic
    placuisti Domino. Alleluia
(Thus have you pleased the Lord.)

Pleased all of us, too. The Cathedral is dominated by two youthful souls, James and Edmund, who could never have imagined its existence, or ours: James the fisherman whom Herod Agrippa executed in AD 44; and Edmund the King of East Anglia who, refusing to share his crown with a pagan, was shot full of arrows, thus making him our Sebastian.

When I got home, wetter than ever, having to walk down the farm track, I reread one of my favourite books, the *General Epistle of St James*, admiring it more than ever, dwelling on its fine passages such as: "Every good gift and every perfect gift is from above, and cometh down from the Father of lights."

That made me think of my old friend Hector Moor, who created the Cathedral lights in his blacksmith's shop. "Behold, we put bits in horses' mouths." And light bulbs in iron hoops.

I fetch in the tender plants for fear of frost. The lawns are a disgrace, nice and mulchy with sodden leaves, over which the white cat picks her particular way, uncaring as to desuetude. This means that they are laid aside as no longer being of use — which cannot be right; for a large part of their utility is in their rotting away, that dark richness of which we are each a part.

James and Edmund, and indeed most of our ancestors until quite recently, mulched all too early. But just watch what grew from them! Yet how could they have imagined it in a thousand Sundays! Two young Christians, one thunderous, the other so quiet that it is a wonder his voice has disturbed history.

It is said uncertainly that Edmund was crowned on Christmas Day on the hillside that I can see from my garden, and that he was 15. The River Stour might have been in flood or frozen, or just idling past the local fishermen. As for James, he would ascend into myth at Compostela.

And now Bishop Nigel from the North has been bound into their holy claims. "We do these things well," said an old gentleman at the tea party.

Should I shop in Bury St Edmunds, I like to take a rest in my stall, to say hello to Matthew the verger and to James and Edmund, to Neil the Dean, to Lillias the artist, to Tony the lifelong friend, and to the old home ground. And, should the rain have stopped, to walk through the carpet bedding that fits so neatly round the ruins, and presumably over Edmund's dust.

The new Bishop dealt wonderfully with James 2.2-3.

Old Money-bags

Tawny gold days with chilly showers. Shrivelled oak leaves on the long lawn. The white cat in her winter chair. Financial mayhem on the kitchen radio. I have been dibbing bulbs in and clearing beds.

The first day of autumn being St Matthew's day, I preach on this reformed taxman at matins. "Old Moneybags" our ancestors called him, because of his attributes in the stained-glass picture.

The entire village smells of Mr Rix's onions, acres and acres of them, grown for the supermarket. It is beautiful. I am still finishing up those that fell from his trucks last year, tugging them from the strings in the larder. Tonight I will pull the popping balsam from the stream, and the water will gather speed. Last night, there were loud owls.

Old friends have celebrated their birthdays: Duncan his 80th, Dodo her 100th — Duncan's in a snowy marquee, Dodo's in a mock-manorial hall at Hadleigh, which, as everybody knows, is an archiepiscopal peculiar. These two gatherings might be said to represent my world: one, farming and the Church; the other, the arts.

They were tremendous feasts, and attended by guests of all generations. Folk from near and far. There were wry speeches, and, at Dodo's party, the candles set off the smoke alarm. How various were their lives. She a girl at St Petersburg, he a boy from Ayrshire.

She walked round the tables on the arm of a tall youth. She wore a rich orange dress and the family garnets, and was her imperious self. We passed a photo of her parents' wedding from hand to hand — a terrace full of prosperous Edwardians with several years to enjoy before the Western Front. Dodo retains their confidence. We sit up when she telephones, never announcing who it is. "Dodo!" we exclaim. Who else?

An entire universe of cousins etc. have arrived. The one I

faced was Jean-Claude, a Protestant lay canon from France. We shout at each other over the plates. At Duncan's lunch, I say an agricultural grace and talk to a dear old man from the fields. He spoke of stooking the sheaves. His face was pale with Time — as was Dodo's — for the years have a way of quietly draining us as the months drain the leaves.

On Thursday, I went to Bury St Edmunds for the cathedral chapter meeting, the country bus wandering extravagantly through parish after parish, my nose pressed to the window to see as much as I could.

Then Bishop Nigel and Dean Neil in the chapter house, then tea, then an extraordinary confession from the Polish taxi-driver on the last phase home. Glancing at me, summing up whether I could take it, young, and, I thought, rather sad, he asked if I was "religious". Adding that he could tell that I was "a gentleman". What next?

Swerving past some cyclists, summoning up his courage, he said that he had seen an angel. Did I believe him? I told him about a great English poet called Blake, who saw angels in Golden Square in London. He told me that he was married and had a little daughter. I praised his English. He was, I thought, about 22 and rather lost. Or maybe found. He was certainly an adventurous driver. There are times when one must be an adventurous listener.

William Blake wrote:

And we are put on earth a little space,
That we may learn to bear the beams of love.

Richard Rolle and Thomas Traherne

There is always a claimant quality in returning to where one once lived, be it ever so long ago. Thus I walk with a lingering sense of ownership around Aldeburgh. The day is dull, and the news on the car radio quite terrifying. So enough of both. And I have a friend to show around, Antony from far Pickering, the Rector of Richard Rolle's lovely church.

We stand by Benjamin Britten's grave. We stroll the Crag Path. We enter the wide aisle where boats were auctioned. We glimpse the sullen marshes where the author of Peter Grimes wondered how he could get away. We mount the Town Steps and plunge over the shingle to see Maggi Hambling's majestic scallop shells fanned out against the steely sea.

We enter the Moot Hall, where the youthful me slept on a camp bed to guard the Millet drawings, and listened to the fall of the waves on to the shingle and scampering rats. We ate fish pie. We pottered around Thorpeness, and I saw in my imagination the memsahibs on furlough, and Empire missionaries taking a break, and boys reading William books, and dads in plus-fours, and the spirit of Sir James Barrie abiding. Never go back, they used to say. But I always go back, if only for lunch.

I have run the lawnmower into the ground, says Mr Walker critically. Heavens, have I? I apologise profusely. He takes it away to mend. I plant a row of purple broccoli, previous neglect of machinery filling my conscience. And then the swans pass over with mighty whooping wings, six of them in rose-white echelon, and I tell myself, why, Mr Walker gains from my hopelessness, so how dare he be cross with me! But he is a man who loves machinery, whose mind joins its mind and, money or no money, he is right to chastise a cack-handed machinery minder such as me. I wring off a fine marrow, pick up a huge apple, and think of — Thomas Traherne.

For it is just 18 years since Richard Birt, then the Rector of Weobley, founded the Traherne Society. Since when his lovely idiosyncratic communications from Herefordshire have alerted the world to the Rector of neighbouring Credenhill, that youthful priest who released the key to Christian delight.

Walking with Richard Birt up to Credenhill Church, Wales falling away to our left, I longed to sing the country clergy, past and present, known and unknown. Parsons like the poet-doctor-priest George Crabbe, who, calling at the Big House and hearing cries of labour, walked upstairs and delivered a fine boy.

And men like Thomas Traherne, who spelled out joy on the page and sent it to a single reader, a married lady veering towards Rome. If Anglican authority wouldn't stop her, then Anglican bliss would. How he loved being alive!

The edges of the great field have been cut. So it looks as though it will be ploughed to the edges. The cyclic forces of food shortage and land prices determine these swathes of grass. Here lies an autumn hay harvest. And here, below the farmhouse, lies a carpet of crab apples.

And here, above it, the badger sett crumbles. And there, a mile away, spreads Suffolk. And now I must give Barry ten pounds for the church cycle-ride, and he gives me the date of the bellringers' dinner. And again the white birds fly past, beating the sky.

A Trip to Cranford

It is the eve of St Luke, and his blissful "little summer" is succeeded by his still blissful rain. Only it pours, softly but relentlessly, just when I have to set out on the last literature festival of the year, this time at Knutsford.

The Euston train slides past Milton Keynes and Stoke on Trent, drenched cities that, unless they hold a literature festival, I may never enter. Watery streaks fly skittishly across the carriage window, and pale shadows flicker on laptops.

I debouch at Macclesfield, another first, where Marie waits to drive me through grand parklands to Mrs Gaskell's Cranford. I should have re-read the novel before I arrived.

It is not remotely as I expected it to be. There she lies in the Unitarian graveyard below an upright cross in an otherwise sloping mass of big recumbent slabs, and, as with Jane Austen at Winchester, not a word on it to say that she was a great novelist. I recall that Mr Brontë broke down the memorial he had erected at Haworth to his genius girls when their readers took to sightseeing.

I tell the literary-festival audience about my life, while the soft rain provides an even accompaniment. How dull it must be to hear. Germaine Greer preceded me — "'Shakespeare's Wife', ticket essential" — and how can I follow either of these ladies? But I press on in my East Anglian way, trusting that face and books will somehow come together in order to make an impact.

Elizabeth Gaskell went to school in Stratford-upon-Avon; so what would she have made of Germaine's version of Mrs Shakespeare? Mrs Gaskell's social, revolutionary even, attitudes were picked up in her childhood from her readings of our stern Suffolk poet George Crabbe. And so the inspired storytelling about the poor and the mighty, the good and the bad, goes on. When we sink back exhausted by the textbooks and the theology, let us continue to find the truth about human life in literature, and in the wonderful storytelling Jesus.

Back to Bottengoms Farm, a miraculous journey of some four hours from soaking Cheshire to the rising Stour. The white cat, who has been greatly moved by that Victorian painting *Faithful unto Death*, in which a hound lies across his master's grave, is waiting for me beneath the walnut tree wet to the skin. She bounds ahead through the garden like a leaping dish-cloth. Soon we are reunited over a little whisky and a lot of Whiskas.

On the table lies my one and only attempt to make a corn dolly. All was going well at the harvest supper when, at the penultimate moment, car keys rattling, Neil the woodman produced his master plan. A handsome figure in horseman's (ploughman's) finery, he walked round the village hall and presented each of us with five corn-stalks, six inches of cotton, and a strip of ribbon. We were to be taught how to make a corn dolly.

These were always made by men. Corn from the last sheaf of the harvest field was woven into a cage where the goddess Ceres could be imprisoned until the following year, thereby ensuring its fertility. The dolly was hung up in the farmhouse.

So we wove as best we could. The Colonel's and my dolly were like a straw version of a lead for a mad dog, but Rosie's — perfection. And at first go. We staggered home at near midnight, sober, worn out, all fingers and thumbs, our vague notions of recent quite ordinary village events brought to a standstill.

With Archbishop Rowan at Lambeth

Christopher and I return from the Gathering (of Lambeth Degree-holders) at the Palace. He has devised a route that I haven't taken since I was a boy: by way of the branch line from Mark's Tey to Sudbury.

The waiting-room, which was identical to the one in which the tentative lovers of Brief Encounter met their guiltless fate, now contains a Coke-and-crisps purveyor, a weary passenger, and a notice to say that we are being watched. Its doors are those through which the businessmen of long ago rushed to get out of the weather, snow on their bowlers. Soon we are rattling across Chappel viaduct, one of the wonders of our world.

As it is half-term, zoo-exhausted children rock on laps. Ten minutes later, we reach Bures, where St Edmund was crowned, and stagger down a bank with a torrent of commuters. Crisp leaves are at our feet; homing rooks are in the shaking branches. I remember the branch lines that shuffle Proust's characters through Normandy, often, as one of his hostesses required, in full evening dress.

Lambeth was October-grey. Plane leaves whirled around the tomb of the Tradescants, court gardeners to the Stuarts. The Thames was steely. The Gatherers filled the Chapel to the brim, and we sang Merbecke and listened to Archbishop Rowan preach on "Whomsoever much is given, of him shall be much required."

We — the Gatherers — have given him the vestments he is wearing. They arrived this very day. He is slight, and has quick youthful movements, and sings the Merbecke in an easy Welsh voice, and preaches like a theological poet, which he is, of course. He sings all the hymns without looking at the book.

Some stand to receive; some kneel. A blind monk and his dog stay wonderfully still. How sacred it all is. The acheiropoietos face of Christ stares down at all of us from its precedence above the altar. This is not the Pantocrator or ruler of all, "but the image miraculously imprinted by the Lord himself on a napkin to be sent to the King of Edessa". I am now quoting from Archbishop Rowan's little book *The Dwelling of the Light*.

Soon it will be luncheon, a wood fire, and summer pudding. Then downstairs where poor Laud and Cranmer would have trod, the stairs still slippery with debate and cruelty, we go to the Crypt.

Here, in 1867, was held the first Lambeth Conference. John Colenso, Bishop of Natal, had created schism just as an American bishop threatens to do now, and Charles Longley, Archbishop of Canterbury (1862-68), summoned it in this hard old room to hear his "Address to the Faithful".

In 2008, Archbishop Rowan's startling prelude to the 18th Lambeth Conference will be three days of Retreat before the debate begins. Listening this week to the hollering Commons, I wondered whether politicians, too, should discover a similar discipline.

But back to the poet at the altar. Having returned to my place, careful so as not to step on the blind monk's dog, and said my thank-you prayer, I recall what Archbishop Rowan said in his book. "Looking at Jesus seriously changes things; if we do not want to be changed, it is better not to look too hard or too long."

Writers are terrific lookers. It is a wonder that their eyes do not burst at all the things they see. The countless faces in the streets, the Face just above their teeming heads, their own faces in its different lights.

Back with Monty in the Desert

The dead are never more alive than during the month they have gone. I am thinking of a good old man who whistled under his breath to announce his approach, and who now lies in a huge silence by the churchyard hedge. This after the young trumpeter from the barracks had blared forth Last Post and Reveille from the rear of the church.

Last thing at night, given a conversational chance, the desert snapshots would appear, the sandy tanks, the grinning lieutenant, Monty in his beret. Alexandria, El Alamein, Sidi Barrani, Tobruk. "That's me." And it would have ended there, were it not that Sergeant Peter gave death a shove. Not yet. Not yet. "He saved my life." The sunburnt bodies, the endless dunes, the unimaginable future. And now no sand, but London clay.

Evensong for Christ the King. Pius XI instituted this feast in his encyclical *Quas Primas* in 1925. How George Herbert would have rejoiced. We sing kingly hymns, and I preach on "Who do men say I am?" Services become alight or do not become alight. This one does. Prayers are said without praying or with praying. These are prayed.

Before this evensong, being early, I wander around, reading inscriptions. They are all cracked and battered by the landmine that fell on the church in September 1940. Here is Mrs Husbands' tomb. She was a Mrs Knight from Chawton, where her descendant would write *Emma* and *Pride and Prejudice*. In my sermon, the confused magistrate asks the strange person in the dock, "Are you a king, then?" November darkness creeps against the coloured glass. The congregation goes home to watch *Cranford*, the lime leaves hissing under its feet. The church goes cold.

Most days at dawn, I use the kitchen window as a view-finder. Drinking tea, being loving to the cat, I allow the glazing-bars to line up the field opposite. It swells like a great breast. Now and then a rider or a walker appears on the horizon like someone in a Western, disturbing the landscape. Paul? One of the girls?

The hazel spreads its branches like fingers to let me see through them. I keep putting off the coppicing. It is so wondrous in its fanning. Squirrels ascend and descend it like Jacob's messengers, and already there are catkin buds. Shakespeare would have been writing *Romeo and Juliet* or *Hamlet* when someone went down the hazels to chop wattle for my walls. All I chop are pea-sticks.

Page-proofs have arrived. This is a nice job, and one not to be hurried. A ruler has to be set under each line to prevent block reading. Other than this, I just read word by word, like a six-year-old. The Indian voice on the telephone wants me to change my ways. It gives a Scottish name. A lady begs my pardon, but could I do an envelope charity collection on my street? What street? A friend says, "Are you busy?" and settles down to a long chat.

The proofs are put on hold. A bit of book comes into my head and has to be written down. "Your head is like a sieve" — Mother. Not true. My head is like an attic, full of things that might come in handy. You never know. People tell me how astonished they are at what it holds. They don't know that there is a cupboard full of questions. But prayer and staring through the breakfast window provide a few answers. Which is a mercy. Or else where would one be?

Vespertillo the Bat

I had a wonderful batman friend in my youth, and how I wish he was here at this moment, so that he could read Natural England's report on our church bat-roost.

He would take me to the bumby-heap in his village at nightfall, where, diving through the thin smoke, we would see one of the world's most misjudged creatures. This year, just as autumn began, came the builders to repair the north-aisle roof.

"It must be finished by 1 December," they said, "to avoid disturbing your bats when in deep hibernation." Not a word about disturbing us. Then Roger and Sylvia arrived to see our bats and pronounce them remarkable.

"Pipistrelle, Brown Long-eared, Serotine and Natterer's bats have been roosting in St Andrew's Church most likely over many years . . . in the void between the ceiling and the roof, and in the wooden joints of the first floor of the tower."

The old boiler-house near the tombs of John Constable's uncles and aunts was probably their dining-room, as it was full of butterfly wings.

We were absorbing this information with self-satisfaction and tolerance, as though we had any choice in the matter, when paragraph 3 descended on us like Nature's PS to the Mosaic law: "You must not deliberately capture (take) or kill a bat. You must not intentionally or recklessly disturb a group of bats. You must not damage or destroy the breeding or resting place (roost) of a bat. You must not possess a bat (alive or dead) or any part of a bat. You must not obstruct access to a bat roost. You must not sell (or offer for sale) or exchange bats (alive or dead), or parts of a bat. . ."

Jonathan, the Species Adviser for East Anglia, then adds:

"Bats depend very much on the goodwill of those involved in church repair."

Advent, and looking up, the scaffolding down, I see that our bats have been given private entrances to their dark kingdom by the Michelmersh Brick and Tile Company. These are 15mm deep, to stop birds joining them.

During all the years I have worshipped in this building, I have never got so much as a squeak out of its bats, although we did find one by the south door after matins and placed it safely by the war memorial.

What did those who created these shrines know of bats? Here is what T. H. White found in a 12th-century bestiary: "Vespertillo the Bat is a paltry animal. It takes its name from the evening (vesper). It has wings, but at the same time it is a quadruped and uses teeth — a thing that one does not usually find in other birds. The Bat parturates like a quadruped, bringing forth, not eggs, but living young.

"Moreover, it does not fly with wings, but is supported by a membrane, poised on which, just as if on a flight of feathers, it moves and weaves about. There is one other thing about these undistinguished animals, and this is that they hang on to each other alternately, and depend from any place like a cluster of grapes. If the top one let go, they would all be scattered. And this they do from a certain duty of affection, of a kind which is difficult to find in man."

The natural history may be dodgy, but the morality puts ours in the shade. How I love that "certain duty of affection". Bats are not blind, as is usually said, but a kind of echo-location guides them through the night. Britain has 12 species, four of which hide their affectionate natures from us as we pray below.

A severe line from Isaiah comes to mind: "In that day a man

shall cast his idols . . . to the moles and to the bats." It means into darkness. But darkness is these creatures' light. It is where they see.

Parson Merman

Frost and a sudden burst of wind not only dislodged what plums remained, but hurled a fraction of the past into the present.

It was long ago, and I was in Cornwall yet again with the poets James Turner and Charles Causley, and there were subtle hints for me to forsake "that cold old Suffolk of yours" and join them in what James, at any rate, called the dolce vita of north Cornwall. And here we were, one mildly wild afternoon, in Morwenstowe, clinging to a cliff in Parson Hawker's parish and shouting, "And shall Trelawney die?"

It was not only the brief gale that blew Hawker into my memory, but the Harvest Festival announcements in church.

As everyone knows, part of Hawker's civilising of his savage folk was his crackdown in 1843 on the traditional Harvest Home, and his institution of the current Harvest Thanksgiving. The former was wilder than the wildest weather — so unmentionable that you won't find a correct account of it in a Thomas Hardy novel. Backs were near-broken, the corn spirit had been safely captured, the drink flowed, and the singing and mating rocked the barn.

Although on 1 August Lammas ("loafmass") bread reached the altar, harvest celebration remained in an earlier religion. Robert Hawker would not have been popular. But then he didn't appear to mind what people thought of him — and, if one shares this trait, one is inclined to sound brave when one is merely doing what one likes.

Where behaviour was concerned, he was more writer than priest, and where saintliness was discerned, he was, well, helpless, as anyone is. As an undergraduate of 19, he married a woman of 41, and they were both entirely happy. Physically, he was somewhat burly, a country clergyman in fisherman's boots with streaming blond hair and a beautiful way with words. When he sunbathed and swam naked, it was assumed that he was a merman.

Hopeless with money, he built himself, all the same, an enormous vicarage, each of the chimneys being in the shape of a favourite church. When his parishioners were not in the fields, they were often up to no good on the rocks, and frightful tales reached his ears.

Their penance was to bring the drowned sailors up to the churchyard and bury them with full Anglican rites. "But supposing they were papists, or, nearly as bad, Mussulmen?" Well, James and Charles and I read Parson Hawker's inscriptions; for each poor Atlantic-soaked body was given a stone. "Unknown — but known."

We, these Cornish friends and I, were at that time very fond of a local historian, Arthur H. Norway. He was the father of Nevil Shute (*A Town Like Alice* — a novel that was partly influential in making my brother an Australian). I find most guides to Devon and Cornwall rather limp stuff after Arthur H. Norway's 1897 guide to those counties in the Highways and Byways series; so I look up his walks in Parson Hawker country.

Being a writer, Norway, in his account of smuggling, tells these stories with less horror than is quite becoming. My favourite is his description of the horses, "shaved from forelock to tail, well-soaked or greased from head to foot, so as to slip easily out of any hostile grasp".

His fame now rests on one of the roots of the current popular myths about the chalice, and on a splendid ballad, "The Song of the Western Men". After his old wife died, he married a half-Polish girl, and became a Roman Catholic on his deathbed.

"To you before the end of Day"

Waiting is a kind of involuntary study. On the station platform, I study the painted iron flowers planted there in 1860. At the bus stop, I study the wild flowers pushing through the lawn-mower's stripes.

In the pub where we agreed to meet, I study faces — only furtively, of course. Should the waiting exceed, shall we say, ten minutes, it will most likely move into a story. Or, at this moment, into some lively natural history; for, from all directions, lapwings are descending on to the winter wheat to take up their crested and monumental positions. Very still, they face the morning sun, no doubt knowing that once they had, all to themselves, an Act of Parliament to protect them; for the farmers were in great debt to them. Now, they just glow.

Meriel then pulls up to take me to the matins for All Souls' and Saints', where I read the sad roll-call, and the familiar figures return to their seats, briefly ousting the present occupants.

Faithful vigil ended,
watching, waiting cease;
Master, grant your servant
his discharge in peace.

Then to Ditchingham, to where all the rural deans of Suffolk have flocked. They are seated in a big circle before the Bishop of Dunwich. Some look perilously youthful. Ditchingham is where Henry Rider Haggard was squire, and where he wrote *King Solomon's Mines* and *She*, and that shocking inventory of the collapse of British agriculture before the First World War, *Rural England*, a tale so dreadful that he prefaced it with a sentence from Judges: "The highways were unoccupied . . . the inhabitants of the villages ceased."

What few good men remained on the blighted fields would soon be mopped up on the Western Front. But the wild flowers would go on growing, and the larks and lapwings would go on descending to their hereditary places.

Compline in the chapel. To you before the end of day, creator of the world, we pray. Then home through the black lanes from the verge of Norfolk to the verge of Essex, where the white cat hangs in a pear tree.

Peter, my publisher, arrives, with a boot-load of books to sign. I wheel them from his car to the house in my second-best barrow. They are, as all out-of-the-bookcase books are, amazingly heavy and profuse.

I am reminded of having to help move Canon Rendall's library when I was about 18. He had died, and the removal men were in his house, and I heard one of them complain: "I don't mind what I do, but I hate having to move a parson. A ton of bloody books before you start!" Pushing the wheelbarrow through the orchard, I tell Peter this ancient whine.

Seated at the kitchen table, I write my name over and over again. Hazel leaves fall slowly against the panes. He has brought me a copy of Sylvia Townsend-Warner's *Somerset*, which he has just reissued. She confesses that "since I am constitutionally incapable of resembling a guide, an err-and-stray-book would be nearer my measure."

At the end, she discovers that she has left out Cheddar cheese and Exmoor ponies. Dear God, forgive our omissions.

Where the Border Shepherds Prayed

To Radnorshire (Powys to the postman) once more, where I have wisely laid down, like a rack of trustworthy wine, a little group of Border friends. It is their Michaelmas festival, and I am to talk on Ploughing. Or, rather, talk between the poetry of ploughing.

This goes back ages to when Langland radically reinvented the Church after the appalling business of the Black Death. A lanky young priest from the Malverns, he put all the English folk who survived into a common field, put all their worship into a barn, and put Christ to the plough. It was only a dream.

The plough poems and prose were read in the Victorian needlework school in Presteigne, where girls were trained to be useful. Brown and gold autumn light filtered through the big windows. Presteigne itself hadn't shifted a step since I was there last October. The same sheepdog rushed at me in the second-hand bookshop; the same damp shine surfaced the streets.

On Sunday, the poet Edward Storey took me to the 11-o'clock, and the sanctuary shone primrose yellow, and there was a fine address on Lazarus and the Beggar. Between festival functions, I read Lytton Strachey's *Queen Victoria* and Edward's new drama on the Last Supper, in which the Thirteen leave the rumpled crumb-strewn table one by one, stressed, wondering, identifying themselves as they thought best. And poor Judas, of course, starting his dreadful career.

And I begin a few days of blissful sloth at Discoed, lolling about between meals in a way that would never be permitted at Bottengoms Farm, picking out the line of Offa's Dyke through the window, admiring three house cats, delving into Edward's library, and waking up at six to see the sheep stirring like wet pearls on the hillside, and rolling to top gear for another day's chewing. Just over the garden wall, the jackdaws are playing cat's cradle on the scaffolding round St Michael's spire.

When I entered this holy, ancient little building, empty of every stick and portable thing, it was Langland's barn all over again. I thought of the Welsh shepherds on their arthritic knees, and heard them singing — in moderate time —

Pleasure it is
To hear, I wis,
The birdès sing.
The deer in the vale,
The corn springing;
God's purveyance
For sustenance . . .

No altar, no sheaves, no whiff of soup such as always accompanies Harvest Festival at Discoed. All this in a nearby loft, an upper room. There Stephen the Rector brought the past and the present, the distant and the near, into logical words. And, afterwards, food and wine in a farmhouse at least as old as any of us could imagine, although the shadowy dogs and villagers, half-lit by sparking logs, suggested *Far From the Madding Crowd.*

And soon, tomorrow, there would be another shepherds' dwelling, Lower Rowley, where David and Judy bred their prize Suffolks, and friends I only met in Radnorshire would appear from low doorways as if it was only last year still. I walked to their oak wood. The tree roots were like rough jewel settings, each group clasping a great rock.